The
ENGAGEMENT
DILEMMA

The
ENGAGEMENT
DILEMMA

How to Create a
Culture of Belonging

DR. ROZ COHEN

MUNN
AVENUE
PRESS

The Engagement Dilemma
How to Create a Culture of Belonging
By Dr. Roz Cohen

First Edition
Copyright © 2025 by Dr. Roz Cohen

Published by
Munn Avenue Press
300 Main Street, Ste 21
Madison, NJ 07940
MunnAvenuePress.com

AVENUE
MUNN
PRESS

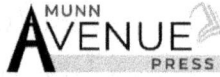

For permission requests, contact MunnAvenuePress.com

Harcover ISBN: 978-1-969679-08-7
Paperback ISBN: 978-1-969679-07-0

Cover Photo by Sarah Deragon

Printed in the United States of America

For my Father, Michael Cohen,
who will always be a guiding presence in my life

For my children, A and M,
who are amazing humans and I am lucky
to have them call me "moomers" or "bruh"
depending on the day

For every Human Resources person
who works tirelessly to create organizations
where people can do their best work....
I see you and you are doing great.

Author's Note on Names, Companies, and Stories

The stories you'll meet in these pages are drawn from my 25-plus years in the HR trenches, leadership research, and spirited "you-won't-believe-this" conversations over far too many cups of coffee. To protect privacy—and to zero in on the lessons that matter—I've blended details, shuffled timelines, changed industries, and swapped identifying traits. Every manager, employee, and organization you encounter here is an amalgamation of real people and real workplaces, but none is a one-to-one portrait of any single person or company.

In plain English: if you think you recognize yourself (or your boss, or your board chair) in these pages, rest assured the resemblance is purely coincidental. The examples are designed to illuminate principles, not to single anyone out. Any errors or oversights are mine alone; the insights, I hope, are gifts we can share.

Contents

Foreword

Understanding, measuring and driving employee engagement in the workplace is one of those topics that is both grounded in decades of good science as well as a perennial "hot topic" with leaders, managers and HR professionals in organizations. We know from years of research as well as our own personal experience (that is, anyone who has ever worked inside a company) that engagement matters. It shows in how you are treated when you apply for a job or are hired by a company. It's evident in the ways in which managers and colleagues work with each other. It's reflected in the types of recognition, reward systems and career offerings available. It's role-modeled in the communications, decisions and behaviors of senior leaders. And it's inherent in the very foundation of the corporate culture.

While engagement has always mattered (although more to some leaders than others), the power of engagement became even more salient during the "great resignation" of the pandemic as employees voted with their feet by leaving companies that showed a true lack of respect or caring for the growth of their people. As corporates are shifting back (or regressing, depending on your perspective) with their emphasis on mandatory Return to Office (RTO) policies, it's easy to see why engagement is, or should be, such a strategic topic in the workplace today.

Given this context, any new book on engagement, and particularly one written during and post the pandemic by a scientist-practitioner who focuses on what works and what doesn't, should be on every leader, manager and HR professional's bookshelf (whether in hard copy or digital form). What makes the Engagement Dilemma stand out above the myriad of other business books in the market, however, is the way in which the author, Dr. Rosalind Cohen, approaches the challenge. We're not talking here about the challenge of just engaging employees. As Roz makes very clear in the book, the Engagement Dilemma is not just about getting people excited about coming to work, but the deeper question and impact of what happens when employees lose faith in their organization and its leaders. While it's true that some employees will decide to exit their organizations on their own in search of a better quality of work life (in the broadest sense), many employees choose to stay and simply actively disengage instead. In post-pandemic language, this is called "quit quitting" and it's a very real phenomenon. Make no mistake, disengaged employees do not bring their best selves to work, deliver their best work, or go above and beyond for the organization. Yet many organizations rely almost exclusively on just a few metrics to measure engagement, including organizational surveys and exit interviews. While these tools are important, and when done well can play a critical role in providing diagnostic information, they are not the solution. Simply measuring and tracking the problem is not the same as doing something about it to drive positive changes in the behavior, practices, and culture of the organization.

That's where the book you have in your hands shines. Through a combination of research, case studies, and personal experiences, Roz focuses on how to build engagement at the individual level of everyday exchanges. Because in the end, leaders and HR professionals can change all the programs, policies, and slogans in the company and still not impact the people who work there. Engagement isn't a simple solve. It's not a one-size-fits-all approach. This is why many organizations are still getting it wrong. In the Engagement Dilemma, Roz identifies the root causes underlying the challenge of engagement and provides tangible actions that anyone (employees, managers, leaders, and HR professionals) can take to enhance the workplace experience. In short, as she points out, this isn't a book about HR practices or measurement models but how to engage with others in a more positive, supportive, and inclusive manner.

But there is much more to the Engagement Dilemma than just content. It's personal. Rarely does one get a chance to read a business book that reflects a sense of purpose and passion in the content being discussed. Having known Roz since she began her dissertation journey years ago, I always knew she was deeply committed to making work more meaningful and positive for everyone. In the Engagement Dilemma, which reflects the culmination of her research and, in essence, her career journey as well, you will learn from her experience as a scientist, practitioner, and human being who cares deeply. This is a powerful book on engagement and one that I hope leaders, managers and employees embrace. Even if you only take away two or three things to do differently in your own interactions with others, you will be making a real difference in the level of engagement you and others experience.

Allan H. Church, PhD
Co-Founder & Managing Partner
Maestro Consulting, LLC
Guilford, CT

How I Got Here

I started writing this book to cash in on my PhD—finally, a practical application for all that theoretical knowledge. I kept writing because people shouldn't need a PhD to like their jobs, though judging by most workplaces, they apparently need something.

After you get your doctorate, writing a book seems like the thing to do.. What better way to show the world you spent a ton of money getting a degree than to create a practical guide used by companies who want to create a culture of belonging and connection.

Then, the universe threw me a plot twist: I realized I was writing another dust-collector that would sit on the shelf next to *Control Everyone with Hypnosis* or *Our Iceberg is Melting*. Cue existential side-eye.

So, the purpose of the book changed. It shifted from "This is what people do who have an academic dissertation" to "How can I actually help people to not hate their jobs?" Because the problem isn't people; it's what we call 'corporate best practices.'

Since then, I have thought of writing this book as a way of connecting my core values of "tikkun olam" (my grandmother's mandate to leave any room better than I found it, conference rooms included) and "tzedakah" (giving back) with the very practical reality that most workplaces are broken in surprisingly fixable ways. It turns out that

Jewish values about making the world a little better wherever you are can apply to conference rooms, just as they do to any community center.

Here's the thing about spending 25 years in HR: you develop a keen eye for spotting patterns. You watch the same preventable mistakes happen over, and over again. You sit through countless meetings where well-meaning leaders discuss "culture" and "engagement" with the same energy they bring to reviewing the quarterly budgets—earnest nodding, furrowed brows, and a group chat about lunch five minutes later.

You also witness those magical moments when someone finally gets it right. When a manager discovers that "How are you doing?" can be an actual question instead of corporate small talk, and then stays to hear the answer. When an organization stops hiring clones and starts building teams that reflect the world we live in. When leaders realize that trust isn't built through team-building exercises involving rope courses and trust falls, but through the daily, intentional choice to see people as whole individuals, not just role-fillers.

The shift in my purpose happened somewhere between watching my fifteenth client implement a surface-level diversity initiative (complete with stock photos of ethnically diverse people shaking hands) and realizing that most of what passes for "employee engagement" in corporate America is about as authentic as a reality TV show.

I started asking different questions. Not "How do we measure engagement?" but "Why are so many people disengaged in the first place?" Not "How do we fix our culture?" but "What would it look like if we stopped breaking it?" Not "How do we retain talent?" but

"Why are we creating environments that make good people want to leave?"

And that's when it hit me: the problem isn't that we don't know what to do. The research is clear. The data is available. The tools exist. The problem is that we keep treating engagement like a program rather than a practice. We keep looking for silver bullets when what we need is bronze consistency.

This book isn't another feel-good manifesto about the power of positive thinking (though I'm generally in favor of both feeling good and thinking positively). It's not a collection of corporate case studies that make everything sound easier than it actually is (though there are plenty of real examples of what works and what spectacularly doesn't).

Instead, this is a field guide for leaders, managers, and HR professionals who are tired of pretending that ping-pong tables equal culture, that annual surveys equal listening, and that "We're like a family here" equals actual care. It's for people who want to do the work—the real work—of creating places where people can thrive, contribute, connect, and maybe even enjoy the eight-to-ten hours they spend at the office (or kitchen table, or co-working space, or wherever work happens these days).

Each chapter builds on research—my own and others'—but always with an eye toward the practical. How do you hire for engagement? How do you onboard people in a way that sets them up for success instead of confusion? How do you manage performance without crushing souls? How do you lead inclusively when you're still figuring out what that even means? The practical approach has led me to create "Tear Sheets" at the end of each chapter, the idea being that even if you don't read the chapter (and of course, I hope you do), you can immediately use the information found there. Think of it as the old school Cliff Notes some of us used to avoid reading anything assigned to us in 11th grade literature class.

You'll also find stories. Lots of them. Because behind every data point is a human being who just wants to do good work and feel valued for it. Some of these stories will make you laugh (including a few where I'm the cautionary tale). Others might make you cringe in recognition. All of them are true, though names and details have been changed to protect both the innocent and the spectacularly guilty.

Fair warning: I'm going to challenge some best practices along the way. The idea that "culture fit" is anything other than bias in a business suit. The notion that you can engage people by measuring them to death. The belief that leadership is a personality trait instead of a learnable skill set.

I'm also going to be honest about what doesn't work, including some of my own spectacular failures. Like the time I called an employee "my pet" in what I thought was an endearing, British sort of way, only to realize I had just made a junior staff member feel like office furniture with emotions. (More on that delightful moment in the conclusion.)

· · ·

But mostly, this book is about hope. Hope that we can do better. Hope that 'endure' and 'career' stop dating. Hope that the time we spend earning a living can also be time spent growing, connecting, and contributing to something meaningful.

Because here's what I've learned after two and a half decades of this work: People don't want much. They want to be seen. They want to be heard. They want to feel like their work matters. They want to be treated like adults who have lives outside the office. They want to grow. They want to belong.

None of this is revolutionary. All of it is achievable.

So, if you're ready to move beyond engagement theater and into the messier, more rewarding work of actually engaging people, keep reading. If you're willing to question some assumptions, try some new approaches, and even admit that some of what you've been doing isn't working, this book is for you.

And if you're looking for quick fixes, silver bullets, or the secret to transforming your culture overnight, this probably isn't the book for you.

For everyone else, let's get to work—no trust-fall required.

Dr. Roz Cohen
San Francisco, 2025

"Connection is why we're here;
it is what gives purpose and meaning to our lives."
– Brené Brown

CHAPTER 1

The Engagement Dilemma

At first glance, FutureTech[1] was a dream employer. With sprawling glass offices in Southern California and a bold mission to "change the world through connected intelligence," it boasted a generous stock plan, unlimited vacation, and ping pong tables on every floor. But beneath the surface, morale was cratering.

It didn't happen overnight. When a round of layoffs blindsided mid-level managers—who had spent the previous quarter rallying their teams for a high-stakes product launch—trust cracked. Not because cuts were made, but because of how it was done: quietly, without acknowledgment, and in direct contradiction to everything the executive team had said in their monthly all-hands meeting.

Then came the engagement survey. Participation dropped to 38%. Results revealed what many had suspected: employees no longer believed leadership had their backs. The phrase "I feel like a cog

---

1 FutureTech is a composite organization based on real patterns I've observed across multiple companies over the years. While the name is fictional, the story is all too real.

in the machine" appeared again and again in anonymous comments. But there was no open-text analysis—no context, just scores. Senior leaders dismissed the data as noise. "The silent majority is happy," said one VP. "It's just a few bad apples making noise."

Except it wasn't. The "bad apples" included some of the most creative minds on the team—the ones still showing up every day, doing the work but quietly browsing job boards over lunch.

What FutureTech didn't realize was that their engagement model had been built like a house of cards. All style, no substance. Yes, there were perks, but no real clarity on advancement. Feedback loops broke down. Managers were overloaded and under-trained. And most critically, no trust existed. When employees don't trust that their feedback will lead to meaningful change, they stop giving it. And when they stop giving it, organizations lose their most valuable early warning system.[2]

It wasn't the first time we'd seen this pattern. Netflix, in its early pivot to streaming, famously declared a "freedom and responsibility" culture. But without consistent manager training or safeguards for psychological safety, that freedom became chaos for some. High performers thrived; others were chewed up by brutal candor and inconsistent standards. Netflix eventually rebalanced, investing heavily in leadership development and clearer performance frameworks, but only after an exodus of exhausted talent.[3]

---

2 Kahn, William A. "Psychological Conditions of Personal Engagement and Disengagement at Work." Academy of Management Journal 33, no. 4 (1990): 692–724.

3 Hastings, Reed, and Erin Meyer. No Rules Rules: Netflix and the Culture of Reinvention. New York: Penguin Press, 2020.

• • •

Zappos, known for its "Holacracy" experiment, went all-in on employee autonomy. The company removed traditional management structures in hopes of unleashing engagement and innovation. What happened instead was a long period of confusion, stagnation, and departures. Without clear accountability or development paths, many employees struggled to see how their work mattered. Culture without structure became chaos. Eventually, Zappos quietly reintroduced managerial guidance, learning the hard way that engagement needs direction, not just good vibes.[4]

And then there are the extreme cases—cautionary tales like Enron and Sun Microsystems. These weren't failures of engagement alone, but the consequences of cultures that prized performance over principle. Employees learned that speaking up was dangerous, not encouraged. Engagement, in these environments, meant aligning with the status quo, even if it led straight off a cliff.[5]

But the real dilemma isn't just failed engagement. It's what companies try to do when they realize something is wrong.

I saw this firsthand. At one firm, the leadership team had fixated on the "bottom 10%" of disengaged employees. They rolled out flashy re-engagement initiatives like free lunches, mentorship programs, and branded hoodies. Meanwhile, they ignored the quiet majority in the middle: the 70% who weren't checked out but weren't fully in

---

4 Greenfield, Rebecca. "Zappos and the Collapse of Corporate Culture." Bloomberg Businessweek, June 2016. https://www.bloomberg.com/news/features/2016-06-15/zappos-and-the-collapse-of-corporate-culture.

5 McLean, Bethany, and Peter Elkind. The Smartest Guys in the Room: The Amazing Rise and Scandalous Fall of Enron. New York: Portfolio, 2003.

either. The ones doing solid work, still open to leaning in if someone would just ask, listen, and lead.

They were trying to save the wrong people. You never solve engagement by throwing perks at the most disgruntled. You solve it by focusing on that middle 70%—the ones who want to believe but need a reason to.

This aligns with a core principle I've seen play out again and again: Engagement isn't binary. It's a spectrum. On one end, you've got the folks who are all in—motivated, invested, aligned with the mission. On the other end? The ones who've mentally checked out but haven't told anyone yet. And then there's the group I always pay the most attention to: the swing voters. The ones who could lean in if the culture, leadership, and systems around them give them a reason to. These are the people you can win over . . . or lose. And once they go, it's hard to get them back.

FutureTech didn't lose people because they had high expectations. They lost them because they broke the psychological contract. Employees expect transparency. They expect to be included in conversations that affect their work. And they expect that when you ask for feedback, you actually listen.[6]

What happened next was predictable. Attrition rose. Referrals dried up. Recruiting costs soared. HR tried to stem the bleeding with culture campaigns and recruitment videos, but the brand damage was already done. It took a near overhaul—new leadership, outside consultants, a long process of rebuilding trust—for things to begin turning around.

---

6 Buckingham, Marcus, and Curt Coffman. First, Break All the Rules: What the World's Greatest Managers Do Differently. New York: Simon & Schuster, 1999.

This is the Engagement Dilemma. Not just the challenge of getting people excited about work, but the deeper question of what happens when they're not. Because disengagement doesn't show up as protest. It shows up as silence. As missed deadlines. As "That's not my job." As the person who used to stay late now logging off the second the clock hits five.

Engagement, real engagement, isn't about beer fridges or branded swag. It's about trust. Clarity. Belonging. And leadership that sees people not just as roles but as full humans: complex, motivated, and capable of extraordinary contribution when they're given the chance.

This book is about how to create that kind of culture, one where people don't just stay because they need the paycheck but because they care about the mission, feel seen in their work, and believe their voice matters.

And it starts with asking the right questions.

I didn't come to this work by accident. My belief in the importance of belonging at work isn't just professional, it's deeply personal. Before I ever sat in a boardroom or built a hiring framework, I was just a kid trying to find my place in a world that didn't always feel safe or welcoming. The questions I ask leaders now—about connection, trust, inclusion—started as questions I asked in my own life. Honestly, I've been building engagement strategies since before I could spell "engagement." So, before we dive into research and strategies, let me tell you where this all began.

As a kid, I grappled with a challenging family dynamic, particularly with my mother. Her narcissism and borderline personality disorder meant that everything revolved around her needs and wants, shaping my entire sense of self from childhood. As I grew older, this experience fueled an intense desire to find genuine connections and a place where I truly belonged. This quest for belonging became a driving force in my life, leading me on a journey from New York to Delaware, then to Oregon, and finally to San Francisco. Each move was a step in my search for something bigger than myself, a place where I could feel comfortable and safe.

My grandmother was a true force of nature who introduced me to Judaism beyond its traditional religious boundaries. Through her, I discovered two powerful concepts: Tikkun Olam and Tzedakah. Tikkun Olam, roughly translated as "repairing the world," asks how we can make the world better as individuals within our society. It's about giving back, about leaving things better than we found them. My grandmother wasn't just talking the talk; she was a real badass. At a time when the field barely existed, she worked in development, raising money for the International House of the Blind in Brooklyn. Her example showed me how these Jewish values could be lived, not just preached.

Even though she died when I was eight, her voice stayed in my head, and I began to understand my feelings of disconnection in a new light. It dawned on me that perhaps the key to belonging wasn't just about finding the right place but about creating connections and meaning wherever I found myself. This realization sparked a burning question that would shape my career: How can I help others feel connected and engaged in their environments, particularly at work?

The question that keeps buzzing in my mind is: How can we create connections that not only fulfill us but also contribute to repairing the world? It's about crafting spaces where people can truly thrive, bringing their best selves to work every day. This isn't just feel-good fluff, but a practical necessity in today's workplace.

As a white woman, I'm acutely aware of my privileges. The concept of Tikkun Olam—repairing the world—pushes me to leverage these advantages for the benefit of others. In my HR work, this translated into opening doors for candidates who didn't have Ivy League pedigrees in a finance sector that typically worships at the altar of prestigious diplomas. I became a bridge builder, forging connections with organizations serving underrepresented groups. The goal? To give talented individuals a shot at roles they might have been overlooked for based on their resumes alone. It's not about lowering the bar, it's about widening the door.

These questions were so compelling that I went back to school for my PhD. My focus was on identity and how we define ourselves. During my studies, we explored two types of identity: surface and deep. Surface identity is what's immediately visible: your skin color, the way you dress, or that unmistakable New York accent I've never managed to shake. Deep identity, on the other hand, is less obvious. For me, it's my Judaism—not something you'd know unless I mentioned it or invited you over for Shabbat dinner.

My research revealed that inclusive leaders exhibit specific behaviors that directly impact employee engagement. And engagement, it turns out, comes in three flavors: affective ("I feel"), social ("I belong"), and cognitive ("I think"). Here's where it gets interesting—a manager's behavior has a direct line to the "I feel" and "I belong" types of engagement. The "I think" part? It's like trying to get a New Yorker to admit Chicago pizza is better . . . not happening.

Thriving or Nose-diving

Some organizations seem to thrive effortlessly while others stall out or spiral. After 25 years in HR across both financial services and non-profits, I've seen a consistent pattern: leadership is the tipping point. The way leaders show up has a direct impact on whether employees feel energized or drained. It's like a seesaw; leaders can elevate teams or send them plummeting with one wrong move.

This got me thinking. Are there leadership styles that consistently lead to positive outcomes? And does a person's identity—you know, the stuff that makes them who they are—play a role in how leadership affects engagement?

So, I rolled up my sleeves and dove into research on inclusive leadership and employee engagement. I initially wanted to focus on the financial sector, but life had other plans. Due to a low response rate (only 11 people . . . yikes!), I had to cast a wider net across various industries. Sometimes, you've got to pivot when the data doesn't cooperate!

Now, here's something interesting: According to recent studies, employees who feel supported by their colleagues and bosses are more likely to be engaged at work. It's not rocket science, right? When people feel valued, they're more likely to give their all.

But here's where it gets juicy. Research has shown a link between social identity and engagement. In plain English, if underrepresented people feel unsupported and unconnected, they're less likely to be committed to their employer. Given our increasingly global society, creating an inclusive environment isn't just nice, it's necessary.

The bottom line? Organizations that empower individuals to embrace their differences are likely to see better outcomes and more engaged employees. It's like creating a workplace orchestra—when everyone's unique instrument is valued, you get a symphony instead of a cacophony.

The U.S. job market today is a pressure cooker. Since the global pandemic, the scramble to attract and retain top talent has intensified (think New York subway platform in August, but with résumés flying.) Companies are battling not just for skills, but for staying power.

Employees want work that challenges them and a workplace where they feel they belong. It's crucial. Companies that can create engaging, inclusive cultures are sitting pretty in this competitive landscape. But here's the million-dollar question: how do leadership behaviors shape these cultures?

To crack this code, my dissertation involved two main questions. Think of it as a double-decker sandwich of data, if you will:

1. Is there a connection between inclusive leadership and employee engagement? (Spoiler alert: there is!)

2. Does this relationship change based on an individual's identity or social group?

After crunching numbers and analyzing responses until my eyes crossed, I found that inclusive leadership is indeed linked to certain aspects of employee engagement. But wait, there's more! This research isn't just for dusty academic shelves. I've whipped up a practical model that HR professionals can use to hire and retain top talent. The following chapters are going to unpack that for you.

During the COVID-19 pandemic, we had a whole generation entering the workforce who'd been cooped up at home for years, their social lives reduced to pixels on a screen. It was like a massive experiment in object permanence—poof, normal life vanished and we all had to believe it would someday return. This hit the younger workforce entrants particularly hard. They hadn't weathered as many storms as older generations, and the uncertainty about whether society would ever return to "normal" left some deep scars. Trust in long-term stability? That's in short supply for these young adults. They're stepping into a world that feels about as stable as a Jenga tower in an earthquake, and we expect them to commit to jobs and industries long-term? Come on. We can't rely on the old playbook of loyalty and engagement. Instead, we need to build cultures that offer a sense of security amidst the chaos.

The way people interact in organizations is heavily influenced by company culture. This fascination with engagement—how employees connect with their company, for better or worse—led me down a rabbit hole. I kept wondering, *How do we build a culture where people feel valued, connected, and like they belong? And more importantly, how do we create this sense of belonging for a diverse workforce?*

When employees see themselves reflected in their manager—same gender, ethnicity, or even just a shared love of terrible puns—their "I feel" and "I connect" engagement levels tend to skyrocket. But even when there's no obvious surface similarity, smart managers can bridge that gap. They create opportunities for people to see beyond the surface, like sharing exercises in staff meetings. Suddenly, people are finding unexpected connections, and those "I feel" and "I belong" engagement levels start climbing faster than the line at a bagel shop on Sunday morning.

Most companies approach hiring with a cookie-cutter mentality. When someone leaves, they dust off the old job description, slap it on a job board, and call it a day. The hiring process then unfolds like this: junior staff handles the opening act (initial interviews), mid-level managers take the second act, and finally, the big kahunas swoop in for the grand finale. It's reactive, it's rushed, and frankly, it's a missed opportunity.

This approach ignores the bigger picture—the organization's evolving needs and culture. It's like trying to solve a Rubik's Cube by only looking at one side. Companies need to ask: What skills are we missing? How does this role align with our strategic goals? It's not just about filling a vacancy, it's about strengthening the entire team.

There are two ways organizations typically tackle this: the "fill the hole" method and the "What do we actually need?" approach. The first is like grabbing the nearest object to plug a leak—quick, but not always effective. The second requires more thought. It asks, "Do we still need someone to do A, B, and C? Or have our needs changed?" This approach challenges the "We've always done it this way" mentality that's as outdated as a flip phone.

The rush to fill positions often leads to a workplace treadmill, running fast but not really getting anywhere. Companies frantically post job ads while overloading existing staff with extra responsibilities (without extra pay, of course). It's a recipe for burnout and missed opportunities. Instead, why not take a breather? Ask yourself: What did this role actually contribute? Is it still relevant? Could technology or a different approach make it obsolete? It's about ensuring the role you're hiring for is the role you actually need.

The Pause

It all boils down to what I like to call 'the pause.' We've been sprinting to fill positions without stopping to ask the real questions. How does this role benefit our company? What else do we need to succeed? The job might be exactly as it was before, but we won't know unless we ask.

Instead of blindly accepting the departing employee's word as gospel, we need to hit pause and talk to the people directly impacted by the role. How do they interact with this position? What do they need from it to keep things moving? Most companies skip this step, diving headfirst into panic mode.

The key is to pause at each stage of the process. When someone resigns, we ask: What role do we truly need? Then we examine our recruiting process. Instead of defaulting to "This is how we've always done it," we consider what makes sense for this specific position. Who needs to be involved in the interview process? What skills—technical, leadership, and social—are essential for success?

Before making the hire, we pause one last time. Have we created a system that truly allows us to find the best person? Have we opened doors for candidates who might not typically have access to this kind of role? Are we breaking down barriers and creating real opportunities?

In our fast-paced world, taking these pauses might feel counterintuitive. But they're critical. They're the difference between perpetuating the status quo and building a truly dynamic, inclusive workforce. So, next time you're tempted to rush through a hire, remember that sometimes, the most productive thing you can do is pause.

This hiring predicament isn't confined to financial services or consulting. It's a universal issue, spanning industries from tech start-ups to local coffee shops. It's as common as rush hour traffic in any major city.

Companies are hiring at breakneck speed. The moment someone leaves, they post a job listing before the dust settles. Everything else becomes secondary, like an afterthought.

We need to consider: Who's actually writing these job descriptions? Are they accurate, or are they as outdated as last year's smartphone? Perhaps the person leaving should write the description. After all, who knows the job better than the person doing it?

We're stuck in old patterns, reacting without much thought. Managers often have their own ideas about the role, which may be far removed from reality. And let's not forget what the organization can support in terms of process. It's like planning a party without checking the budget.

What if we asked the person leaving to help write the job description before they go? It might seem unconventional, but it could provide valuable insights.

Ultimately, it's about clarity. Clarity around vision, mission, expectations—the whole package. Without it, we're just guessing and hoping for the best. And frankly, that's no way to run a business in today's competitive landscape.

Next up in Chapter 2, we're going to dive into the nitty-gritty of employee engagement and why it's crucial for your organization's success. We'll explore the tangible benefits of engaged employees and the hidden costs of disengagement.

In Chapter 3, we'll discover how inclusive leadership can transform your workplace culture and boost engagement. We'll break down the key behaviors of inclusive leaders and how they impact different aspects of employee engagement.

We'll learn strategies to attract top talent in a competitive job market in Chapter 4. We'll also explore innovative recruitment techniques and how to craft job descriptions that resonate with your ideal candidates.

Chapter 5 is all about onboarding effectively and how to set up new hires for long-term success and engagement. We'll discuss how to create an onboarding experience that goes beyond paperwork and truly integrates new employees into your culture.

Chapter 6 zeroes in on navigating the challenges and opportunities of engaging remote workers. We'll explore tools and techniques to foster connection and collaboration in virtual environments.

In Chapter 7, we'll take a peek into the future of engagement with AI and emerging technologies. We'll discuss how AI can enhance engagement strategies and the potential pitfalls to watch out for.

Chapter 8 will focus on exploring emerging trends and future predictions in employee engagement. We'll discuss how to stay ahead of the curve and adapt your engagement strategies for the workplace of tomorrow.

In Chapter 9, we'll reflect on how organizations can move from insight to action, especially when engagement has gone off track. Through real-world examples and personal lessons, we'll examine what it takes to rebuild trust, re-center your culture, and support leaders in becoming more inclusive and adaptive. You'll learn how to course-correct without starting from scratch, and how small shifts in leadership behavior can lead to lasting, systemic change.

Stick around. It's going to be a fun ride.

The Bottom Line

Engagement isn't binary—it's a spectrum. Focus on the middle 70% (your "swing voters") who want to believe in your company but need a reason to. Most companies waste resources trying to save the bottom 10% while ignoring those who could be won over.

Immediate Actions You Can Take Today

Diagnose Your Current State

- **Survey participation audit**: If engagement survey participation is below 60%, you have a trust problem, not just an engagement problem

- **Exit interview analysis**: Look for patterns in departures—are you losing creative minds who are still showing up but quietly job hunting?

- **Manager load check**: Are your managers overloaded and under-trained? This breaks feedback loops faster than anything else

The Pause Protocol

When someone resigns, implement these three pauses:

Pause 1: Role Assessment

- Don't immediately post the same job description

- Ask: "What did this role actually contribute?" and "Is it still relevant?"

- Talk to people who directly interact with this position

Pause 2: Process Design

- Question: "Who needs to be involved in interviews for THIS specific role?"
- Identify essential skills: technical, leadership, and social
- Challenge "we've always done it this way" thinking

Pause 3: Opportunity Creation

- Ask: "Have we opened doors for non-traditional candidates?"
- Consider: "Are we breaking down barriers or perpetuating them?"

Focus on the Right Metrics

- **Track the middle 70%**: Create specific engagement initiatives for employees who are neither fully engaged nor completely checked out
- **Monitor psychological safety**: Can people speak up without fear? This is your early warning system
- **Measure trust indicators**: Do employees believe feedback leads to meaningful change?

Leadership Behavior Checklist

- **Transparency**: Include employees in conversations that affect their work
- **Follow-through**: When you ask for feedback, show how you're acting on it
- **Clarity**: Provide clear advancement paths and expectations
- **Belonging**: Help employees see connections beyond surface-level similarities

Red Flags to Watch For

- Declining survey participation (especially under 50%)
- Comments about feeling "like a cog in the machine"
- Managers dismissing feedback as "noise from bad apples"
- Increasing "that's not my job" responses
- People logging off exactly at 5 p.m. who used to stay late

Quick Wins

1. **When possible, have departing employees write their own job descriptions** before they leave
2. **Ask three people** who work with a departing employee what they actually need from that role
3. **Stop throwing perks at disengaged employees—** invest that energy in the middle 70%
4. **Create "connection opportunities"** in team meetings for people to find unexpected commonalities

The Engagement Spectrum Reality Check

- **Top 20%**: Already engaged—don't over-invest here
- **Middle 70%**: Your biggest opportunity—focus here
- **Bottom 10%**: Likely too far gone—don't waste resources trying to save them

*"Customers will never love a company
until the employees love it first."*
– Simon Sinek

CHAPTER 2

Cracking the Code of Engagement: Why it Matters

People often ask me how I went from running HR teams in high-pressure financial firms to earning a PhD focused on inclusive leadership and engagement. The truth is, I was trying to solve a puzzle I'd been staring at for over two decades. A puzzle that refused to go away.

In my 25 years of working in HR, across everything from Wall Street firms to nonprofits, I kept seeing the same patterns. A new leader would come in, full of vision, talking about "culture" and "retention" like they were items to check off a to-do list. Engagement surveys would roll out with great fanfare. Consultants would be brought in. Sometimes there'd be bean bags in the breakroom or "unlimited" PTO policies. And then, within months, reality would sink in: good people were still leaving. The ones who stayed were disengaged. And no one seemed to know why.

But I had a hunch.

It wasn't that people didn't want to be engaged. It's that we weren't building workplaces where they *could* be. Where they felt safe. Where they felt seen. Where they belonged.

And I couldn't stop wondering, *What makes people feel truly connected at work? What kind of leadership actually moves the needle? And does who you are—your identity, your background, your lived experience—change how you engage?*

Eventually, these questions pushed me out of the boardroom and into a PhD program. I wanted real answers backed by research, not just gut instinct. My dissertation explored two core questions:

1. Are the dimensions of Inclusive Leadership (IL) related to aspects of Employee Engagement (EE)?

2. Are there differences in the relationship between IL and EE by individual or social identity?

These questions weren't abstract for me. They were rooted in every story I'd collected from employees who whispered their truths after meetings. From managers who wanted to do better but didn't know how. From high performers who left not because they weren't challenged, but because they felt invisible.

As I dug into the research, I uncovered something that confirmed what I'd always known intuitively: Engagement isn't just about doing the work. It's about feeling *something* while doing it. Feeling like you matter. Feeling like you're part of something bigger than yourself.

Here's where things got really interesting: The data showed that inclusive leadership behaviors—things like treating people fairly, valuing their unique perspectives and identity, and creating space for belonging—had a statistically significant impact on the *affective* and *social* dimensions of engagement. In plain English? How leaders behave can directly influence whether people feel good at work and feel like they belong.

The cognitive piece was trickier. It turns out that people can stay intellectually stimulated by their work even when they don't feel particularly valued or connected. But that doesn't mean they're sticking around for the long haul.

In many ways, my research gave language to what I'd seen for years: Great leadership doesn't mean having all the answers. It means creating the kind of environment where people feel safe asking hard questions. Where differences aren't just tolerated but *welcomed.* Where who you are deep down doesn't have to be left at the door.

I also explored the idea of identity in the workplace - something we rarely talk about honestly in most HR departments. Through my work, I began to distinguish between **surface identity** and **deep identity.** Surface identity is the stuff you can see: race, gender, age, and how someone dresses. Deep identity is less visible: religion, trauma, neurodivergence, values, and passions. You wouldn't know I was a survivor of incest just by looking at me. Or that I knit to calm my nervous system. These aren't things that show up on a resume. But they shape how I show up at work.

And here's the thing: when people feel they can't bring those parts of themselves to work—or worse, that those parts will be used against them—they disengage. Quietly. Sometimes permanently.

The organizations I studied weren't failing because they didn't have the right strategy or vision. They were failing because they didn't know who their people *really were*. Or how to lead them accordingly.

What I learned along the way is that you can't "crack the code" of engagement with a survey or a slogan. You have to listen. You have to build trust. And you have to do it over, and over again, especially across lines of difference.

The good news is there is a code. And it's not magic. It's methodical. Inclusive leaders ask questions. They hold space. They admit what they don't know. And they model vulnerability—not performatively, but consistently.

This chapter, and indeed this whole book, is about translating what I learned, both in practice and through research, into tools leaders can actually use. Because engagement isn't a "nice to have." It's the difference between teams that thrive and teams that quietly fall apart.

And for me, it's personal. I've spent my career trying to build the kind of workplaces I needed when I was coming up in the world. Where people don't just survive, but *belong*.

And once I started seeing engagement this way—not just as output, but as energy—it changed everything. The most engaged employees weren't the ones being micromanaged into compliance. They were the ones drawn in by purpose, by recognition, and by feeling that their work mattered. They lit up when given the space to thrive. And that led me to a powerful realization: Maybe engagement isn't something we build so much as something we cultivate. Something people lean toward when the environment is right.

Ever notice how plants stretch toward the sun? It's not just a neat botanical trick, but a fundamental principle called heliotropism. All living things, including us humans, are drawn to positive energy. We're like walking, talking sunflowers, constantly orienting ourselves towards what makes us feel good and alive.

Now, let's bring this idea into the workplace. Think of engagement as the professional version of heliotropism. It's what happens when employees are drawn to their work like plants to sunlight. They're not just showing up, they're blossoming.

But here's where things get a little messy. Ask ten different HR gurus what "engagement" means, and you'll get eleven different answers. Gallup, the folks who love to measure everything, say it's about being "involved in, enthusiastic about, and committed to work and workplace." Willis Towers Watson, not to be outdone, calls it "the willingness and ability to contribute to company success."[7] And Aon Hewitt throws in their two cents with "the level of an employee's psychological investment in their organization."[8]

Are you confused yet? Join the club. The HR world has been tossing around terms like "personal engagement," "work engagement," and "job engagement" like hot potatoes. It's enough to make your head spin faster than a desk chair with a loose screw.

Let's rewind to where this all started. Back in 1990, a smart cookie named William Kahn decided to figure out what makes people show up at work. Not just physically, but mentally and emotionally too. He came up with two ideas: "personal engagement" and "personal disengagement."[9]

---

7 Haiilo. (2024, May 27). 10 employee engagement statistics you need to know in 2024. Haiilo Blog. https://blog.haiilo.com/blog/employee-engagement-8-statistics-you-need-to-know/

8 Aon Hewitt. (2018). 2018 Global Engagement Report. Aon.

9 Kahn, W. A. (1990). Psychological conditions of personal engagement and disengagement at work. Academy of Management Journal, 33(4), 692-724.

Personal engagement is when you bring your whole self to work—body, brain, and feelings. It's like showing up to a party in your favorite outfit, ready to mingle and have a great time. Personal disengagement, on the other hand, is more like attending that same party in a full-body armor suit. You're there, but you're not really there.

So, why should we care about all these engagement mishigas (aka craziness)? Simple. When people are engaged, magic happens. Work becomes more than just a paycheck; it becomes a place where people thrive, innovate, and actually enjoy spending their time and contributing to the company's success. And let's face it, we spend way too much time at work not to enjoy it, right?

Then there is the specter of employee burnout, the evil twin of engagement.

Back in 2001, a trio of researchers (Maslach, Schaufel, and Leiter) decided to flip the script on engagement by looking at its opposite.[10] They came up with a three-headed monster of burnout:

1. Exhaustion: Picture yourself as a wrung-out sponge, too drained to even think about work.

2. Cynicism: This is when you start seeing your job through Grumpy Cat memes.

3. Inefficacy: The feeling that you couldn't accomplish anything meaningful, even if your mom was cheering you on.

But enough doom and gloom. Let's talk about the good stuff.

---

10 Maslach, C., Schaufeli, W. B., & Leiter, M. P. (2001). Job burnout. Annual Review of Psychology, 52, 397-422. https://doi.org/10.1146/annurev.psych.52.1.397

In 2002, Harter and his colleagues looked at nearly 8,000 business units across 36 companies.[11] Their verdict? Engagement isn't just feel-good fluff. It's linked to real business outcomes like customer loyalty, profitability, and even safety. Ka-ching!

A few years later, Dr. Alan M. Saks jumped on the engagement bandwagon. He found that engaged employees are not only more satisfied with their jobs, but they also go above and beyond. We're talking organizational superheroes here, folks. They are those people who willingly take on that extra assignment, stay late because they are committed to the project's success, or organize the after-work get-together for the team.

Saks' research[12] unveils key factors driving engagement. It boils down to employees feeling valued, having meaningful work, and perceiving fairness in the workplace. Essentially, when an organization invests in its people, those people are more likely to invest their energy and talents back into the organization.

Macey and Schneider take a more nuanced approach, viewing engagement as a three-part construct:

- **Trait engagement:** An individual's inherent disposition towards work.
- **State engagement:** The emotions and attitudes stemming from that disposition.
- **Behavioral engagement:** The actions that result from these thoughts and feelings.

11 Harter, J. K., Schmidt, F. L., & Hayes, T. L. (2002). Business-unit-level relationship between employee satisfaction, employee engagement, and business outcomes: A meta-analysis. Journal of Applied Psychology, 87(2), 268-279. https://doi.org/10.1037/0021-9010.87.2.268

12 Saks, A. M. (2006). Antecedents and consequences of employee engagement. Journal of Managerial Psychology, 21(7), 600-619.

Crucially, they argue that leadership and job design play pivotal roles in shaping each of these aspects. It's a delicate balance, where each element influences the others.

This research underscores that engagement isn't merely a trendy HR term. It's a complex, multifaceted concept with real-world implications for workplace success. As we delve deeper, we'll explore why hiring for engagement is more than just a smart strategy; it's a fundamental approach to building a thriving, dynamic workplace where employees genuinely want to contribute their best efforts.

At the end of the day, employee engagement is the Holy Grail of any successful organization or business (it doesn't matter if you are making widgets or saving the world). It's that elusive concept that, when achieved, supposedly makes everything in your organization run smoother than a well-oiled machine. But let's dig deeper into why it matters so much.

Imagine an organization where people genuinely enjoy what they do, where they bounce out of bed in the morning excited about work. These engaged employees feel a sense of purpose and value. They're part of an organization that supports them, giving them that warm, fuzzy feeling of belonging, connection, and inclusion. And the cherry on top? They're producing the goods or services that keep the organization thriving. Sounds perfect, right?

But here's the rub: it's not that simple. Engagement isn't a one-size-fits-all concept. It's as unique as your grandmother's secret recipe for noodle kugel. Each person has their own engagement 'flavor,' and it needs to align with the organization's culture. When it doesn't, you end up with sporadic or mixed engagement, like a Spotify playlist on shuffle that doesn't quite flow.

Now, if you ask 45 different experts what engagement means, you'll get 45 different answers. But in my research, I noticed some common themes. There's intentionality—engagement doesn't just happen by accident. It's directed towards either the job or the organization's culture. But here's where it gets fuzzy: What does engagement look like? Is it the person burning the midnight oil, or are they just inefficient? Is it going the extra mile on a project, or just basic competence?

Now, let's talk about what engagement looks like when it's done right. I've found that engagement falls into three buckets:[13]

1. Positive Cognitive Engagement (PCE):

The "I think" aspect.

2. Shared Social Engagement (SSE):

The "I connect" or "I belong" feeling.

3. Positive Affective Engagement (PAE):

The "I feel" component.

Let's zoom in on that last one—Positive Affective Engagement. This is all about how you feel about your actual work. It's that spark of excitement when you sit down at your computer or step onto the factory floor. It's the enthusiasm for the tasks you do every day. In my research, I asked people three key questions: Do you feel positive about your work? Do you feel energetic about it? Do you feel enthusiastic about it?

---

13 Cohen, R. F. (2022). The relationships between dimensions of inclusive leadership and aspects of employee engagement: Crucial connections for organizational success [Doctoral dissertation, Antioch University]. AURA. https://aura.antioch.edu/etds/871

Let's explore disengagement. As I said before, it's like the evil twin of engagement, lurking in the shadows of your workplace. There are three main culprits behind employee disengagement, three external variables that can turn your vibrant workforce into a sea of glazed-over eyes and half-hearted efforts.

First up, we have circumstances. This is when the work or the environment is misaligned with what employees want or expect. It's like showing up for a salsa class and finding out it's actually a line dancing session. The godfather of engagement research, Kahn, defines disengagement as when people "withdraw and defend themselves physically, cognitively, or emotionally during their role performance."[14] Picture employees mentally checking out, browsing Amazon instead of working, or turning a coffee break into a two-hour gossip session.

But the biggest villain in this disengagement drama? Drum roll, please . . . it's manager behaviors. Yes, how managers act can make or break employee engagement faster than you can say "TPS report" (Thank you Office Space) It's the feeling that your manager is hindering your work, blocking your connection to others, or misaligning you with the organization's culture. Think unclear directions, micromanagement, lack of recognition, or unfair treatment. It's like trying to run a marathon with your shoelaces tied together—frustrating and ultimately futile.

---

14 Kahn, W. A. (1990). Psychological conditions of personal engagement and disengagement at work. Academy of Management Journal, 33(4), 692-724. https://doi. org/10.5465/256287

Understanding these aspects of engagement and disengagement is crucial. It's not just about making people happy (though that's a nice bonus). It's about creating an environment where people can thrive, innovate, and drive your organization forward. In the next chapter, we'll dive into how inclusive leadership can combat disengagement and foster these positive forms of engagement.

So, what is the secret code of engagement? The stuff that turns a job into a calling? First up, we have the "I belong" factor. It's that warm, fuzzy feeling of connection, of shared values and goals. It's about finding your work BFFs—you know, those colleagues who make Monday mornings bearable.

Imagine this: You're grabbing a coffee, and instead of beelining back to your desk, you swing by your work buddy's station for a quick chat. It doesn't matter if you're in different departments or working on separate projects. This connection transcends the org chart. It's about feeling part of something bigger than your to-do list. That is the feeling of belonging—having relationships with others based on the work you do or some commonality you share (think pickleball team).

Now, let's switch gears to cognitive engagement—the "I think" part of the equation. This is where your brain gets its workout. It's about being laser-focused on your tasks, paying attention to the nitty-gritty details of your projects. It's what gets you jumping out of bed in the morning, excited to fire up your computer and tackle that challenging problem.

You might be thinking, *Wait a minute, isn't this similar to positive affective engagement?* Good catch! They're like fraternal twins—related but distinct. Affective engagement is all about feelings, while cognitive engagement is about thinking. It's the difference between "I feel excited about this project" and "This project challenges me intellectually."

Think of it this way: Affective engagement is the heart of your work experience, while cognitive engagement is the head. One makes you feel good about your work; the other makes you think deeply about it. When both are firing on all cylinders, that's when the magic happens.

Understanding these nuances isn't just academic navel-gazing. It's the key to creating a workplace where people don't just show up but show up ready to give their all.

But hang on for a sec . . . think about what could cause your company to fail before you even begin in the engagement arena. If you said, "job descriptions," you win the prize. You know—those often dry, long, and sometimes misleading snippets that are supposed to entice top talent. Companies tend to treat these crucial documents like an afterthought, slapping together a list of responsibilities and qualifications without much thought to the bigger picture. If you are a person who is job hunting, you're looking for that spark of excitement, that intellectual stimulation that makes you think, "Yes, this is what I want to be doing!" But too often, there's a disconnect between what's written in the job description and what the job entails. It's like ordering a gourmet meal and being served a microwave dinner—it's technically food, but not what you were expecting.

This mismatch creates an engagement gap right from the get-go. Companies are missing a crucial opportunity to set the stage for engagement before an employee even walks through the door. It's like they're stumbling at the starting line of the engagement race.

Most companies' hiring processes are as outdated as renting a VHS from Blockbuster. Here's how it usually goes down: Someone leaves, and the knee-jerk reaction is to dust off the old job description, maybe give it a quick once-over, and then hand it off to HR with a "looks good to me" shrug.

Then, the posting goes live. In big companies, an HR person sifts through resumes like they're speed-dating profiles, judging who makes the cut. In smaller outfits, it might be someone in the department playing resume roulette. Either way, candidates are shuffled through interviews with the same tired questions that have been asked since the dawn of time (or at least since the company was founded).

The truth is that organizations have more control over this process than they realize. They can influence the culture, shape the work environment, and guide how managers behave through reinforcement and rewards. They have the power to make that first impression count by crafting job descriptions and hiring processes that genuinely reflect the essence of the role and the company culture.

Too often, however, they're not seizing this opportunity. They're not digging deep enough to ensure that what candidates think the job will be aligns with reality. It's a missed chance to lay the groundwork for engagement from day one.

Remember The Pause, which we discussed in the last chapter? The reflection doesn't stop there. Once you've nailed down what the role should be, it's time to think about how you're going to find the right person. Are your interview questions revealing what you need to know? Or are they just checking boxes on a form that's been photo-copied so many times it's barely legible?

Next, we'll get into how to ask questions that cut through the noise and surface to reach the things that actually predict success: adaptability, growth mindset, and cultural alignment. Because in today's workplace, it's not just about what a candidate can do today, but who they can become tomorrow.

The Bottom Line

Engagement has three distinct dimensions: "I feel" (emotional), "I belong" (social), and "I think" (cognitive). Leadership can directly influence the first two, but cognitive engagement requires intentional hiring and role design. To succeed at engagement from the start, rethink your job descriptions and hiring processes.

The Three Faces of Engagement

"I Feel" (Positive Affective Engagement)

- Excitement about daily tasks and projects
- Energy when sitting down to work
- Enthusiasm for the actual work being done

"I Belong" (Shared Social Engagement)

- Connection to colleagues beyond departmental lines
- Feeling part of something bigger than individual tasks
- Shared values and goals with team members

"I Think" (Positive Cognitive Engagement)

- Intellectual stimulation and challenge
- Deep focus and attention to detail
- Mental workout that keeps you engaged

CHAPTER 2 CRACKING THE CODE OF ENGAGEMENT TEAR SHEET

Immediate Actions You Can Take Today

Apply The Pause to Every Role

Before posting any position:

- **Ask:** Do we still need this exact job?

- **Evaluate:** What has changed since the last person was in this role?

- **Define:** What does success look like now (not what it looked like before)?

- **Revise the job description and include the** hiring manager, top performer, and HR in the discussion

Transform Your Job Descriptions

- **Stop**: Dusting off old job descriptions and posting them as-is

- **Start**: Crafting descriptions that spark intellectual excitement

- **Include**: What someone will actually be doing day-to-day

- **Highlight**: Growth opportunities and challenges

- **Test**: Would this description make YOU excited to apply?

Create Manager Peer Circles

- **Form small groups** of 4-6 managers

- **Meet monthly** to troubleshoot real engagement challenges

- **Share strategies** that actually work

- **Commit to trying** one new approach each month

- **Follow up** on what worked and what didn't

Revamp Your Interview Process

Ask questions that reveal:

- **Adaptability**: "Tell me about a time when your role completely changed"

- **Growth mindset**: "What's something you taught yourself recently?"

- **Cultural alignment**: "What kind of work environment brings out your best?"

- **Engagement drivers**: "What made you most excited to come to work in your last role?"

Quick Diagnostic Questions to ask yourself and your colleague/team/executive leadership

For "I Feel" Engagement:

- Do people seem energetic about their daily tasks?

- Are team members enthusiastic when discussing projects?

- Do people volunteer for challenging assignments?

For "I Belong" Engagement:

- Do people hang out together beyond required meetings?

- Are there cross-departmental friendships?

- Do employees refer candidates to open positions?

For "I Think" Engagement:

- Are people asking thoughtful questions in meetings?

- Do employees seek out learning opportunities?

- Is there evidence of deep work and focus?

Remember: Surface vs. Deep Identity

- **Surface identity**: What you can see (race, gender, age, dress)
- **Deep identity**: What's hidden (values, experiences, neurodivergence, trauma)
- **Create space** for people to bring all parts of their identity to work
- **Don't assume** you know what motivates someone based on surface identity

Critical Success Factors

1. **Treat engagement like a strategy, not a survey**
2. **Own it**: Assign clear accountability for engagement outcomes
3. **Evolve continuously**: The work world is shifting—your approach must too
4. **Start before hiring**: Engagement begins with how you attract talent
5. **Manager development is non-negotiable**: They're your engagement multipliers

Red Flag: Job Description Test

If your job descriptions read like legal documents instead of exciting opportunities, you're already losing the engagement battle. Great descriptions should make qualified candidates think: "I need to work there."

*"Diversity is being invited to the party;
inclusion is being asked to dance."*
– Vernā Myers

CHAPTER 3

Inclusive Leadership:
The Game-Changer You Need

Once upon a time, there were two women I worked with—both brilliant, both accomplished, and both sitting in positions of real power. Let's call them Thelma and Louise. Same level, same org chart box, wildly different experiences for anyone who had to report to them.

Thelma was one of those rare leaders who could walk into a room and instantly make it feel like the air got lighter. She didn't pretend to have all the answers, and she didn't need to. She made space for other people's ideas. She knew when to step back, when to ask questions, and when to say, "You know what? I don't know, but let's figure it out together." If you were in a meeting with Thelma, you knew your voice would be heard, even if you were someone who usually kept quiet. She was intentional about it. She'd send agendas out in advance, ask quieter folks for their thoughts, and make sure that decisions weren't just made by whoever spoke loudest.

Louise . . . was a different story.

Look, I like Louise now. I really do. Time softens the edges. But back then? Working for her was like walking on a tightrope over a pit of lava, while she shouted at you from the sidelines about how you weren't holding the pole right.

Louise believed she always had the right answer, even when the topic was way outside her expertise. She'd dominate meetings, talk over people—especially if they disagreed—and shoot down alternative ideas before they even hit the table. I'd be explaining a complex HR issue, and she'd cut in to explain it *for* me . . . incorrectly. If you challenged her publicly, you could expect subtle retribution. Not in a big, dramatic way, but you'd find yourself left off the next project, or mysteriously ineligible for the bonus you thought was coming. There was no brave space, no open dialogue, and certainly no sense of belonging unless you happened to agree with her.

Now here's what's wild: both women thought they were being good leaders. Both were smart. Both were passionate about their work. But only one created an environment where people could thrive.

This, to me, is the heart of inclusive leadership.

And if you're picturing this as some sort of "nice to have" soft skill, let me stop you right there. Inclusive leadership behaviors aren't about being nice. It's about being *effective*. It's the difference between a team that merely survives and one that innovates, collaborates, and gets stuff done without the emotional hangover.

During my doctoral research, I started to dig into this at a deeper level. I wasn't just interested in whether someone *felt* nice to work with; I wanted to know what inclusive leadership actually *looked like* in practice, and whether it could be measured. And I found that it can.

I found five key behaviors that inclusive leaders exhibit consistently:

1. **They seek out dissenting voices**, not just the ones who nod along like bobbleheads.

2. **They create space for productive conflict** and don't treat disagreement like insubordination.

3. **They tackle their own biases first**, instead of assuming bias is everyone else's problem.

4. **They get comfortable being uncomfortable,** especially when conversations get real.

5. **They prioritize authentic participation** over superficial harmony because real ideas live beyond the script.

Thelma did all of this without making a show of it. She ran meetings and made decisions in a way that told everyone, "Your voice matters here." Louise, on the other hand, saw alternate opinions as threats. That created a culture of cautious silence, and we all know nothing innovative ever comes out of a room full of people too scared to speak.

These stories stuck with me because I realized something that, frankly, a lot of orgs still don't want to admit: we are promoting the wrong people into leadership.

We reward technical expertise—who's best at the numbers, who's most polished in front of a client—but we forget that managing people is an entirely different skill set.

That's why I don't treat inclusive leadership like a personality trait. It's a practice—one that can be taught, modeled, and reinforced. But only if we truly value it and hold people accountable to it.

Back in Chapter 1, I introduced the three core dimensions of engagement:

- **Cognitive** ("I think") – how intellectually absorbed someone is in their work

- **Affective** ("I feel") – how emotionally positive they feel about it

- **Social** ("I belong") – how connected they feel to others and the organization

In my research, I took this further, studying how inclusive leadership influences each of these areas. What I found confirmed what I'd suspected all along: Inclusive leadership has the greatest impact on the emotional and social aspects of engagement. It's what helps people feel good about what they do and with whom they do it. And let's be honest: that's exactly where many leaders struggle most.

It's not enough to delegate tasks or assign responsibilities with a tidy RACI chart[15] and call it a day. (Though I do love a good RACI when it's done well.) If people don't feel seen or heard, they're not going to do their best work, no matter how clearly you've defined who's "responsible" versus "accountable."

And inclusive leadership can be learned. I know because I've helped organizations do it. I've seen firsthand how learning inclusive

---

15 RACI is a common project management framework used to clarify roles and responsibilities. The acronym stands for Responsible, Accountable, Consulted, and Informed. See: Project Management Institute. A Guide to the Project Management Body of Knowledge (PMBOK® Guide), 6th ed. (Newtown Square, PA: PMI, 2017).

leadership transforms not just individual managers but entire teams. But theory only gets you so far.

It's one thing to talk about this in theory. It's another thing to walk into an organization and see what happens when inclusive leadership is missing. The gap becomes painfully obvious—not in a spreadsheet, but in the silence that hangs in meetings, the tension in emails, the burnout that no wellness program can fix. I've seen this play out more times than I can count.

I once worked with a nonprofit whose senior leadership team was as siloed as different apps on your phone—each member doing their own thing with no integration. The executive director was charismatic but allergic to feedback. Her team was overwhelmed, disjointed, and terrified of speaking candidly in meetings. The vibe? More courtroom than collaboration.

We started small. I introduced a weekly leadership "pulse check," where team members were invited to share, anonymously at first, one thing that was working and one thing that wasn't. The goal wasn't to create a vent session. It was to teach the executive team to listen without defending. Over time, we shifted meeting structures, rewrote performance review criteria to include inclusive leadership behaviors, and held real-time feedback workshops.

Six months in, one of the most reserved leaders on the team said to me, "This is the first time in years I feel like what I say matters."

That's inclusive leadership in action. Not because it was perfect, but because it created space for people to show up differently.

Inclusive leadership isn't just another corporate buzzword destined for the jargon graveyard alongside "synergy" and "paradigm shift." Let's talk about the word "inclusion" for a moment. This word has gotten some very bad press lately and has become very politicized. I think of inclusion as making sure everyone feels valued for who they are, the experiences they bring, and their ability to contribute. It's not always about feeling comfortable—growth and connection come with discomfort—but it's about creating spaces where everyone can participate fully and know they belong. At its core, inclusion is about honoring our shared humanity and desire to be part of something meaningful.

Inclusion is a fundamental approach to leading teams by actively seeking out and valuing different perspectives. Think of it as creating an organizational potluck where everyone brings their unique dish to the table—and trust me, you haven't lived until you've seen what happens when someone brings both a kugel and kung pao chicken to the same meeting. (Much better than serving the same bland corporate casserole day after day, which reminds me suspiciously of the mystery meat in my high school cafeteria.)

The real secret to inclusive leadership is that, like any good family recipe, it needs to be baked into your organization from the start, not just sprinkled on top as an afterthought. The data shows us that when organizations authentically embrace different perspectives, starting with their hiring practices, they see measurable improvement across every metric that matters: innovation, problem-solving, employee satisfaction, and yes, the bottom line. McKinsey's research found that companies in the top quartile for ethnic and cultural diversity were 36% more likely to have above-average profitability. That's not just food for thought; that's a whole feast of evidence.

At its core, inclusive leadership requires leaders to step up and advocate for their team's diverse needs and values. It's about creating spaces where people feel safe enough to contribute without feeling like they need to put on a corporate mask or check their identity at the door. Because let's face it, pretending to be someone you're not at work is as exhausting as maintaining a poker face at a family reunion.

This approach transcends the outdated notion of diversity as merely a legal checkbox or quota to fill. Instead, it embraces a more profound truth: Equality isn't just nice to have; it's essential for creating systems that work for everyone. It's like upgrading from a bicycle to a motorcycle. Sure, they both get you there, but one is clearly more evolved than the other.

The real power of inclusive leadership lies in its ability to remove obstacles that keep some people stuck in the corporate equivalent of the kids' table. We're talking about developing genuine skills in relationship-building, collaboration, and creating workspaces where everyone can thrive. It's about building partnerships and consensus in ways that engage everyone meaningfully, and not just the usual suspects who dominate every meeting like it's their personal TED talk.

This takes work, the kind of work that might make you uncomfortable sometimes. But that's the point—growth rarely happens in our comfort zones, and the best leaders understand that discomfort often precedes progress. The payoff is a workplace where innovation flourishes because everyone brings their best ideas to the table, not just their best impression of what they think a professional should be.

The path to meaningful organizational change demands more than symbolic gestures and carefully worded press releases. The murder of George Floyd in 2020 forced businesses to confront an uncomfortable truth: We must choose between performative allyship and genuine leadership transformation.

"Othering" infiltrates organizational culture with the stealth of a seasoned corporate politician. While it occasionally appears in obvious forms, like discriminatory policies or biased comments, its most insidious manifestation lies in subtle behaviors. A casually mispronounced name here, an unconscious dismissal of non-elite credentials there. These micro-behaviors create macro-problems.

Inclusive leadership stands as the counterforce to this divisive dynamic. However, it requires more substance than the typical corporate response of forming committees or scheduling annual diversity workshops. Real inclusive leaders cultivate "brave spaces",[16] environments where people are encouraged to engage in open, honest, and challenging dialogue as well as embrace discomfort and vulnerability as essential components of learning and growth, also known as environments where growth edges comfort. Think of it as the difference between karaoke practice in your shower and performing on stage—both involve singing, but only one pushes you to real improvement.

---

16 Arao, B. & Clemens, K. (2013). From safe spaces to brave spaces: A new way to frame dialogue around diversity and social justice. In The Art of Effective Facilitation: Reflections from Social Justice Educators, ed. L. M. Landreman. Sterling, VA: Stylus, pp. 135-150.

Defending the Senior Leader

I still remember the day I caught myself in full defender mode. I was co-facilitating a leadership lab when our CFO casually quipped that "the data team members are just glorified number-punchers." Without thinking, I found myself mentally rationalizing his remark: "Well, he's under pressure . . . he probably didn't mean it that harshly."

That's when a second voice piped up: "Hold on. Why am I giving him the benefit of the doubt?" In that instant, the very bias I was teaching about slapped me in the face. I paused the session and invited the group to unpack what had just happened. I confessed that my reflexive defense of a senior leader had more to do with my own affinity bias—my tendency to protect someone I'd worked with for years—than any thoughtful appraisal of his comment.

Together, we ran a quick "bias check": What assumptions did we bring into everyday conversations? Whose perspectives were we privileging without realizing it? That moment became the springboard for deeper self-awareness exercises throughout the chapter—proof that real inclusive leadership begins not with grand gestures but with the courage to question our knee-jerk loyalties.

The foundation of inclusive leadership rests on self-awareness, particularly regarding affinity bias. This unconscious preference for people who mirror our own experiences shows up in countless decisions. The former athlete who naturally connects with other sports enthusiasts in interviews. The Ivy League graduate who instinctively favors candidates from similar institutions. Recognition of these patterns marks the first step toward dismantling them.

Five key behaviors distinguish truly inclusive leaders:

- They pursue dissenting voices with the enthusiasm of a detective chasing leads

- They nurture environments where productive conflict catalyzes innovation

- They tackle their own biases before addressing those of others

- They embrace discomfort as growth's necessary companion

- They value authentic participation over superficial harmony

These characteristics aren't optional extras in modern leadership; they're as essential as financial acumen or strategic thinking. The Chauvin verdict demonstrated that systemic change becomes possible when we summon the courage to examine our own biases and assumptions. The question isn't whether to embrace inclusive leadership but how quickly we can master its principles.

An example of failed leadership

Working with a healthcare startup provided a front-row seat to what happens when good intentions collide with poor leadership. Despite their noble mission of addressing healthcare inequities, this team of ten talented professionals found themselves trapped in an organizational structure that made the DMV look streamlined.

The root problem was a cultural foundation built on that most dangerous of corporate clichés: "We're one big family." While this sounds warm and fuzzy, in practice, it often translates to "We expect unlimited dedication with minimal boundaries"—about as healthy as using chocolate cake as a breakfast staple. The founder, despite repeated attempts to define this fuzzy cultural vision, remained obsessed with controlling minute details rather than building a sustainable culture.

The result was a masterclass in how not to lead. Highly qualified professionals needed permission for even the most basic office supplies. The approval process involved five different sign-offs and could take weeks. The founder's micromanagement extended to absurd levels. Rather than trusting the team's judgment on simple tasks like document handling, they required detailed status updates on every minor step. This wasn't just inefficient, it was demoralizing for a group of experienced professionals who had been hired for their expertise.

The organizational fallout was predictable. Meetings became optional social gatherings, office relationships deteriorated faster than week-old lettuce, and productivity plummeted. My HR role transformed from standard administrative duties into something closer to organizational therapy. Employees weren't climbing

Maslow's Hierarchy of Needs; they were stuck in the basement, searching for basic psychological safety with a broken flashlight.

This case study serves as a perfect negative example, the leadership equivalent of a "what not to wear" guide. It proves that inclusive leadership requires more than just mouthing the right platitudes about diverse perspectives and inclusion. Real inclusive leadership demands concrete actions that empower employees to bring their best selves to work, rather than their most obedient selves.

Consider this a cautionary tale, a reminder that the road to organizational dysfunction is often paved with well-intentioned but poorly executed leadership philosophies. The next section will explore how to build truly inclusive environments, where trust and autonomy aren't just buzzwords in a mission statement but daily realities.

An example of good leadership

A global non-profit guided by core values such as respect, integrity, and advocacy transformed inclusion from a PowerPoint bullet point into living and breathing organizational DNA. This 1,000-person organization examined what prevented their employees from feeling connected to an inclusive environment that promotes physical, mental, and spiritual well-being.

Their methodology combined rigorous structure with adaptable leadership principles. Quarterly training sessions focused on practical servant leadership applications, moving beyond surface-level corporate workshops. Leaders tackled concrete challenges: managing complex conflicts, fostering diverse perspectives, and creating environments that encourage authentic self-expression. The results spoke for themselves. As managers implemented these principles, they saw a clear shift from basic compliance to genuine engagement. Employee contributions became more substantial and meaningful. The traditional right-wrong dynamic transformed into a more sophisticated approach where collaborative learning became the norm. This led to measurable improvements in both team performance and individual growth.

What makes this approach stick is its focus on concrete managerial competencies. They're not just developing leaders; they're cultivating ambassadors of belonging who spread these practices throughout the organization with the effectiveness of a well-designed viral campaign. The change isn't superficial. It seeps into every organizational crevice, creating lasting transformation.

This type of organization excels in its approach to workplace conflict. Instead of avoiding disagreements or forcing artificial harmony, they've turned conflicts into opportunities for innovation and change. They equip their leaders with practical tools and clear protocols for managing productive discourse. Their message is clear: diverse perspectives are essential to success, not just nice-to-have additions. What makes their approach effective is its practicality. Rather than promoting vague concepts about workplace harmony or enforcing superficial positivity, they provide specific frameworks for managing tension. Leaders receive concrete training in facilitating difficult conversations, which consistently turns potential conflicts into collaborative breakthroughs. The results are measurable: improved team dynamics, better decision-making, and more innovative solutions.

This methodology rests on a fundamental truth: Inclusive leadership isn't about eliminating conflict but harnessing its creative potential. Think of it as teaching leaders to conduct an orchestra rather than silence the instruments. By establishing clear rules of engagement, they've created an environment where different opinions emerge naturally and contribute meaningfully to decision-making.

This creates a workplace where disagreement doesn't trigger defensive postures but sparks genuine dialogue. Diverse perspectives aren't just invited to the table but are expected to bring their full flavor to the feast of ideas. It turns out that when you teach people to dance with differences rather than tiptoe around them, the whole organization moves with considerably more grace and purpose.

The five core behaviors identified above distinguish leaders who successfully cultivate engaged organizations. I've seen these practices transform even the most entrenched corporate cultures, particularly in environments where processes have hardened into unexamined habits—rather like that mysterious container in the break room refrigerator that's been there since the Obama administration.

The first behavior might surprise you. While many organizations cling to the "We've always done it this way" mantra, inclusive leaders dare to question everything. They approach legacy processes with healthy skepticism, examining each practice with the thoroughness of a detective at a crime scene rather than accepting "tradition" as a valid excuse.

Moving to the second behavior, these leaders revolutionize meeting dynamics. I've watched countless meetings unfold like a one-person show with a perpetual supporting cast, but inclusive leaders recognize that silence often masks structural barriers rather than a lack of interest. They've taught me that what looks like disengagement usually signals something deeper. They adapted their approach to something simple and refreshingly practical. They distribute agendas in advance, giving introverts time to prepare, rather than expecting improvisational brilliance. Meeting protocols establish participation as a fundamental expectation, not an optional exercise. Follow-up documentation ensures ideas don't evaporate once the meeting ends.

I've found the most impactful element is how these leaders actively pursue dissenting voices, particularly from those traditionally relegated to the organizational margins. They understand that silence doesn't equal disengagement any more than a quiet library signals an absence of thought. Through individual follow-ups and tailored communication approaches, they create multiple channels for diverse perspectives to surface.

The result is that meetings transform from procedural theater into genuine collaboration forums. In my experience, this systematic approach does more than just increase participation; it ensures diverse viewpoints shape organizational decisions, creating solutions as rich and varied as the people who contribute to them.

The essence of workplace psychological safety runs deeper than your typical diversity handbook suggests. I've found it's about creating environments where people can bring their authentic selves to work without turning the office into a daytime talk show. Speaking from experience, as a Jewish mother of two from New York, every facet of who we are shapes how we show up professionally. My characteristic New York directness and enthusiastic hand gestures (which, yes, have turned virtual meetings into what appears to be an impromptu game of charades) become assets when channeled properly.

Case Study: Bossard's Military Commanders

In a 2017 qualitative study, Bossard observed frontline military commanders navigating life-and-death decisions while simultaneously cultivating a climate of trust, openness, and psychological safety among their troops. One commander, Captain Reyes, received intel that a key supply convoy was at risk of ambush. Rather than issuing a top-down order and retreating behind secure lines, she gathered her lieutenants and sergeants for a rapid "weather-check" huddle.

She began by inviting each leader to voice worst-case scenarios: "What could go wrong if we push forward?" Then she flipped the script: "How might we adapt if the road is clear, or if it's blocked?" By surfacing every concern, from equipment failure to troop fatigue, she signaled that every perspective mattered, regardless of rank. This collective problem-solving session lasted fifteen minutes, but it transformed the unit's mindset. Soldiers felt seen and heard; they volunteered to scout alternate routes, devised contingency plans, and even identified local civilian liaisons for fresh intelligence.

When the convoy rolled at dawn, they advanced with far greater cohesion than a simple command-and-control order could ever inspire. The ambush never materialized, but more importantly, Captain Reyes had demonstrated that inclusion under pressure isn't a "nice-to-have," it's mission-critical. Embedding this ethos into your own teams can yield the same payoff: agile responses, higher trust, and a sense of shared ownership, even when the stakes couldn't be higher.

We all carry what I like to call our personal "baggage collection" into work—those life experiences and characteristics that influence how we operate professionally. The trick isn't unpacking every suitcase (your colleagues don't need a detailed update on your cat's gluten sensitivity or your teenager's social media drama) but rather creating spaces where relevant aspects of our identities can meaningfully contribute to our work.

This is where inclusive leaders earn their stripes. They build what I call the "container of trust," a framework for having those challenging conversations while maintaining professional boundaries. Think of it as establishing house rules for healthy disagreement: all the structure of a diplomatic summit but without the formal wear and mind-numbing protocols.

I've seen masterful inclusive leaders orchestrate this delicate balance. They set clear expectations for interaction, acting less like traditional bosses and more like skilled conductors, ensuring every instrument in the orchestra gets its moment while maintaining harmony. Their secret? Creating an environment where differing viewpoints energize rather than derail progress.

The real art lies in calibration—encouraging authentic expression while keeping things professional. When it's done right, you get a workplace where diverse perspectives spark innovation instead of tension. It's not about lowering standards but about raising possibilities by allowing people to bring their full professional selves to the table.

Nothing tests your professional courage quite like hearing a senior leader casually write off talent with a comment like "They went to a state school. How smart can they be?" (This was actually said by a senior leader.) A remark that landed with all the grace of a piano falling from a tenth-floor window. I found myself at that classic career crossroads: speak up and risk ruffling some very expensive feathers or stay quiet and let bias masquerade as business judgment.

I chose to speak up. Instead of nodding along, I initiated a conversation about why someone might choose a state university. The reasons proved illuminating: financial realities, family circumstances, being first in their family to attend college—none of which had anything to do with intellectual capacity.

This discussion birthed what I call "threshold attributes," a smarter way to evaluate talent. Rather than obsessing over where candidates got their degree, we focused on what actually matters by looking at those who have demonstrated success. For example, when leaders learned that the most successful people in their organization were curious, communicated effectively, or demonstrated integrity, we looked at the behaviors that showed attributes. Suddenly, we were measuring what counts instead of counting what's easy to measure.

The shift wasn't simple. Convincing people to look beyond the comfort of prestigious diplomas felt like asking them to navigate without their favorite compass. But we kept pointing out an obvious truth: a fancy degree no more guarantees great performance than an expensive suit guarantees executive gravitas.

We developed rigorous methods to assess actual capabilities rather than institutional pedigree. Yes, it required more effort than simply scanning resumes for Ivy League degrees. But the results spoke volumes. We started finding incredible talent in places our old system would have overlooked (Stay tuned as there is more to come about this later.)

This experience taught me something crucial about inclusive leadership: Sometimes you have to be willing to challenge sacred cows, even when they're grazing in the executive pasture. Real organizational change often starts with one person willing to ask, "But why do we assume this is true?" Even when—especially when—the answer seems obvious to everyone else in the room.

The Bottom Line

Inclusive leadership isn't about being nice—it's about being effective. It directly impacts the "I feel" and "I belong" dimensions of engagement. The difference between teams that survive and teams that thrive often comes down to whether leaders create psychological safety and harness diverse perspectives for innovation.

The Five Core Behaviors of Inclusive Leaders

1. Seek Out Dissenting Voices

- Actively pursue perspectives that challenge the status quo
- Don't just accept the "nodding bobbleheads"
- Create multiple channels for diverse viewpoints to surface
- Follow up individually with quieter team members

2. Create Space for Productive Conflict

- Treat disagreement as innovation fuel, not insubordination
- Establish clear protocols for healthy disagreement
- Turn tension into collaborative breakthroughs
- Teach people to "dance with differences" rather than avoid them

3. Tackle Their Own Biases First

- Recognize affinity bias (preference for people like yourself)
- Question knee-jerk loyalties and assumptions
- Implement regular "bias checks" in decision-making
- Model vulnerability by admitting when you're wrong

4. Get Comfortable Being Uncomfortable

- Embrace discomfort as growth's necessary companion
- Create "brave spaces" where challenging dialogue happens
- Push beyond superficial harmony to authentic engagement
- View growth edges as opportunities, not threats

5. Prioritize Authentic Participation Over Superficial Harmony

- Value real ideas over scripted responses
- Encourage people to bring their professional selves to work
- Create "containers of trust" for meaningful conversation
- Focus on what people contribute, not just how they comply

Immediate Actions You Can Take Today

Transform Your Meetings

- **Send agendas in advance**: Give introverts time to prepare

- **Establish participation expectations**: Make engagement non-optional

- **Create follow-up protocols**: Ensure ideas don't evaporate after meetings

- **Rotate speaking opportunities**: Don't let the same voices dominate

- **Ask specific people for input**: "Sarah, what's your take on this?"

Implement "Threshold Attributes" Evaluation

Instead of relying on pedigree, focus on behaviors that predict success:

- **Curiosity**: How do they approach new challenges?
- **Communication**: Can they explain complex ideas clearly?
- **Integrity**: Do their actions match their words?
- **Adaptability**: How do they handle change and uncertainty?
- **Collaboration**: Can they work effectively with diverse perspectives?
- **Or other attributes that work within your organization**

Create Productive Conflict Protocols

- **Establish ground rules**: Disagree with ideas, not people
- **Time-box discussions**: Prevent endless debates
- **Assign devil's advocate roles**: Systematically challenge assumptions
- **Document different viewpoints**: Show all perspectives are valued
- **Follow up on decisions**: Explain how diverse input shaped outcomes

Build Psychological Safety

- **Admit your own mistakes publicly**: Model vulnerability
- **Ask "What could go wrong?"**: Invite worst-case scenarios
- **Celebrate productive failures**: Learn from experiments
- **Check assumptions**: "Help me understand your thinking"
- **Create anonymous feedback channels**: Remove barriers to honesty

Warning Signs of Non-Inclusive Leadership

- Meetings dominated by the same voices

- Ideas shot down before full explanation

- "We've always done it this way" as default response

- Defensive reactions to feedback or questions

- Silence treated as agreement

Critical Success Factors

1. **Challenge senior leadership when necessary**: Inclusive leaders push for better, even upward

2. **Move beyond comfort zones**: Growth happens in "brave spaces," not safe spaces

3. **Focus on contribution over credentials**: Evaluate what people actually bring, not where they came from

4. **Make inclusion operational**: Build it into processes, not just values statements

5. **Model the behavior**: Inclusive leadership starts with your own actions, not your team's compliance

CHAPTER 3 INCLUSIVE LEADERSHIP: THE GAME-CHANGER YOU NEED TEAR SHEET

"You've got to just say, 'I want the best talent.'...
if you go for the best talent and have the employee base
in your company reflect the available talent outside,
you will actually end up with a diverse pool."
– INDRA NOOYI

CHAPTER 4

Magnetizing Talent: How to Attract the Best

Hiring is one of those things everybody thinks they're good at. Like driving. Or remembering the words to songs from your childhood. But after two decades in HR, let me tell you that most organizations approach hiring with all the nuance of a sledgehammer.

Take one of the firms I joined early in my career—a prestigious asset management company split between New York and San Francisco. Smart people, high expectations, shiny branding. But when it came to attracting talent? The place had a revolving door of sameness. They were looking for "top-tier" talent, which mostly meant Ivy League grads who knew how to use Excel and had strong opinions about Cabernet.

The problem wasn't just that it lacked diversity; it was that they didn't even notice it lacked diversity. Their idea of a qualified candidate had quietly ossified into a narrow type: same schools, same backgrounds, same "polish." So, when I suggested we step back and ask who succeeds here, not just who looks good on paper, you would've thought I had asked if we could replace the conference room coffee with instant coffee from a vending machine.

But I persisted.

We dug into performance reviews, manager feedback, exit interviews, and engagement surveys. We didn't just ask, "Who's doing well?" We asked, "Why?" What are the qualities our best performers share?

After months of digging, a pattern emerged. The top performers weren't just those with the fanciest résumés. They had something else—something harder to quantify but impossible to ignore. They had what I came to call threshold attributes, traits like intellectual curiosity, adaptability, integrity, and the ability to build trust quickly across a range of personalities and power dynamics.

So, we rebuilt our hiring process around those three buckets:

- **Skills** – Can you do the job?

- **Leadership potential** – Can you help others do the job?

- **Threshold attributes** – Can you thrive in this culture and help it evolve?

The results were immediate. We started asking different questions in interviews—more behavioral, less hypothetical. Instead of asking, "What's your biggest weakness?" (which no one answers honestly anyway), we asked, "Tell us about a time you challenged the status quo, and what happened next." That question alone told us more about someone's actual values than a whole stack of references ever could.

And yes, this led to some surprising hires.

The image of an 'ideal candidate' often becomes organizational DNA, with leadership's biases influencing hiring decisions at every level. It's not that they're seeking a specific person, but rather a type—someone who fits their predetermined mold, shaped by both organizational culture and, let's be honest, a healthy serving of unconscious bias. These preconceptions act like invisible walls, blocking potentially excellent candidates from even entering our field of vision.

This reality hit home for me years ago when reviewing resumes for an entry-level financial services position. Among the stack of predictable, fresh-faced college graduates landed something different: an application from a New York City doorman in his early thirties. His background was non-traditional compared to what we were used to seeing come across our desks. He was state school-educated, had had a meandering career path, and his current role manning the front door of a Manhattan apartment building was anything but typical. My first thought wasn't about his qualifications but about how the hiring managers would react. The standard "requirements" read like a corporate mad lib: bachelor's degree, finance experience, team sports background . . . you know, the usual suspects. On paper, our doorman candidate checked some boxes but definitely charted his own course on others.

And once we had that, we stopped chasing unicorns and started looking for real people who brought real value.

Let me also say this: the "hire someone you'd want to be stuck in an airport with" metric? That's not a hiring strategy. That's a BuzzFeed quiz. Friendly and familiar don't automatically translate to competent and creative. Some of the best hires I've made were people I wouldn't necessarily vacation with, but they were phenomenal collaborators, sharp thinkers, and generous teammates.

Hiring for engagement isn't just about who fits the culture; it's also about who can shape it for the better.

And it's on us, as leaders, HR folks, and hiring managers, to widen the door. Because if we only ever recruit from the same places, we'll keep getting the same results. The same blind spots. The same resignation letters six months later, when someone realizes they were hired for what was on their resume, but not for who they really are.

It's not about lowering the bar. It's about clarifying what the bar is. Can they do the work? Will they bring value to the team? Do they exhibit the threshold attributes we know drive success in this culture?

This chapter is about helping you build a system that does just that—one that magnetizes the right talent instead of filtering it out before it even has a chance. It's about knowing what matters, having the discipline to define it clearly, and the courage to question your assumptions. Because the best people for the job might not be the ones you expect.

They'll be the ones you remember.

$$\cdots$$

So how do we break out of that mold? How do we widen the lens and create hiring systems that surface real potential, not just pedigree?

That's where intentional design comes in. Because if we don't challenge the defaults, they'll keep running the show, quietly shaping who gets seen, who gets hired, and who never even makes it past the resume screen.

· · ·

This got me thinking about what really makes someone successful in an organization. I've found it comes down to three distinct buckets. First, there are skills—the basic toolkit needed to perform the job. Second, leadership potential—which, contrary to popular belief, isn't something you need to be born with any more than you need to be born knowing how to use Excel.

Threshold attributes are the keys to cultural success. As I mentioned in the last chapter, these attributes are crucial differentiators in hiring because they are characteristics you can't teach, like intellectual curiosity and integrity. These fundamental traits distinguish exceptional hires from competent ones, yet they're often the hardest to assess in traditional interviews.

If these three buckets are what truly matter, then why should we care whether someone developed their people skills greeting residents at a luxury apartment building or schmoozing clients at Goldman Sachs? Excellence doesn't wear a particular pedigree. In our doorman's case, his job required exceptional communication skills, the ability to work with people across all social strata, and quick problem-solving abilities—precisely the attributes our organization valued.

Looking for these essential attributes during hiring is like being a detective who follows the evidence rather than jumping to conclusions. Whether someone developed their skills in an Ivy League lecture hall or the lobby of a luxury apartment building shouldn't matter more than their actual capabilities. Yet too often, we let surface credentials act as shortcuts for real assessment.

Though he ultimately wasn't hired, the doorman's story cracked open something more valuable than a single position - it sparked a conversation that needed to happen. Like a small pebble creating ripples in a pond, his application challenged our organization's autopilot approach to hiring. We began shifting from "You must fit this cookie-cutter mold" to "Show us who you are and what you can bring."

Take intellectual curiosity, for instance. It's an attribute prized by organizations like a rare gem, and for good reason. Curious people are the ones who look at a process that's been gathering dust since the Clinton administration and ask, "But why do we do it this way?" They're the ones who keep organizations from calcifying into museums of "We've always done it this way."

But here's the thing about attributes like curiosity: they don't check your diploma before taking up residence in your personality. They don't care if you developed them while writing a thesis at Harvard or solving complex customer service challenges at a front desk. What matters is that they're there, ready to be put to use.

The challenge for organizations is to develop hiring processes that can spot these attributes regardless of their packaging. It's about looking past the surface details that too often act as proxies for potential: the name of your university, your zip code, or whether your last name sounds like it belongs on a building. Because excellence, like truth, doesn't care about pedigree.

At the organization I discussed earlier, success seemed more like folklore than fact; everyone had a different theory about what worked. Determined to uncover the truth, I spent six months conducting in-depth interviews with employees at every level. This comprehensive study revealed clear patterns about what actually drove exceptional performance.

After this deep dive (which felt part social science experiment, part corporate anthropology), I emerged with ten clear threshold attributes—the DNA of success in our culture. But identifying these traits was just the appetizer. The main course involved rebuilding our entire talent management system around these characteristics. We transformed our hiring process from a traditional "check the boxes" exercise into something more nuanced. Sure, we still needed to know if candidates could wrangle spreadsheets or navigate specific software. But alongside these technical assessments, we added questions that probed deeper: "Tell me about a time you saw a process that made as much sense as a screen door on a submarine, and how you constructively challenged it."

This system did something remarkable. It started stripping away the unconscious biases that typically cling to hiring decisions like barnacles on a boat. Instead of relying on gut feelings or superficial credentials, we had concrete criteria that actually predicted success.

Think about team meetings, for instance. If asking questions gets you the same reception as suggesting pizza with pineapple, people quickly learn to keep quiet. But in an environment where curiosity is celebrated, it becomes contagious. The key is recognizing that intellectual curiosity, like any attribute, comes in different flavors. One person might express it through rapid-fire questions in meetings, while another quietly researches and presents detailed analyses. An inclusive leader understands that both approaches add value; they're just different paths up the same mountain. The real breakthrough comes when you align these success attributes with how people think about their roles. It's like creating a matching system that pairs the right talent with the right environment, not based on surface-level credentials but on the substantive qualities that drive success. Because at the end of the day, identifying great talent isn't about checking credentials, but about recognizing potential, wherever it might appear.

Getting the Dance Right

My research revealed something fascinating about inclusive leadership: it's like a key that unlocks two specific doors in the workplace. When leaders demonstrate inclusive behaviors (think fair treatment, openness to differences, and fostering authentic connections), employees feel more connected to their colleagues and more enthusiastic about their work (what we previously called "I belong" and "I feel"). It's not rocket science, but it is social science.

The relationship between leaders and their teams isn't some cold, mechanical transaction. It's more like a dance where both partners constantly adjust and respond to each other. When people share work values and goals, it creates a sense of belonging that's as comfortable as your favorite coffee mug. Over time, these relationships build trust and respect, creating what we call "brave spaces" (Arao and Clemens, 2013)—environments where people feel safe enough to share different viewpoints without fear of being thrown under the proverbial bus.

While inclusive leadership significantly influences how people feel about their work and connect with colleagues, it doesn't affect what I call "cognitive engagement" (aka "I think" engagement), that laser-focused attention people bring to their tasks. Think of it this way: Some people are just naturally wired to be detail-oriented and focused, regardless of who's running the show. As one participant put it, "I am intrinsically motivated and passionate about the work I do." It's like having an internal engine that runs regardless of external conditions.

This discovery suggests something crucial for organizations: Instead of managing every aspect of engagement, focus on finding people who naturally bring cognitive commitment to their work.

To get to the heart of cognitive engagement, ask interview questions like these:

- Was there a time you were motivated to solve a complex problem or improve a process at work? Why? What drove you to do so?

  ▸ **Why ask this?** It checks for intrinsic drive and internal motivation.

- How do you take on a task that requires deep focus and creative thinking? Give an example of when you invested significant thought into improving a task or process.

  ▸ **Why ask this?** It explores how the person can be intellectually absorbed in their work and their capacity to think critically about improvements.

- Can you tell me about a time when work got tough, maybe because of a challenging environment or tricky relationships with others? How did you stay focused and get things done?

  ▸ **Why ask this?** This determines whether engagement is internally driven and resilient to external influences.

- What's something about your personal values or how you like to work that pushes you to do your best? When did those values show up in your work?

  ▸ **Why ask this?** This identifies whether engagement stems from their values, internal sense of purpose, or another reason.

- Have you thought about ways to improve your work or your team's work, even outside of work hours? Can you share an example of something you came up with?

  ▸ **Why ask this?** This gauges whether candidates naturally invest mental energy into their work.

Meanwhile, invest in developing inclusive leaders who can create environments where people feel valued and connected. Because while you can't manufacture internal motivation, you can certainly create conditions where it thrives.

The implications are clear: Inclusive leadership isn't just a nice-to-have management style; it's a crucial factor in creating workplaces where people feel genuinely connected and enthusiastic about their work. But it's also important to recognize its limitations. Some aspects of engagement come pre-installed in your employees' operating systems, and no amount of external tinkering will fundamentally change that.

When I talk about hiring practices in organizations, I concede that it is possibly the greatest corporate gamble since casual Friday was introduced. Despite HR's best efforts to create foolproof interviewing systems that reduce bias and ensure candidate fit, the truth is that hiring remains about as predictable as weather forecasting. Companies do their best to match the right people with the right roles at the right times, but it's still largely educated guesswork wearing work-appropriate attire.

The debate around interview styles ranges from the absurd to the rigid. On one end, you have companies asking candidates what kind of cat they'd be (I wish I were joking). Google and Apple became famous for their brain-twisting interview questions that seemed more appropriate for a philosophy class than a job interview. On the other end, you have highly structured processes that, while about as exciting as plain oatmeal, help reduce bias by ensuring everyone faces the same questions in the same order.

Then there's the eternal debate: who should conduct first-round interviews? Some argue for junior staff to do initial screening, while others insist senior leaders should take the first pass since they know what they're looking for. But having your top brass conduct 20-30 initial interviews is like asking your CEO to personally greet every visitor at reception—theoretically ideal but practically impossible.

However, there's a method to this madness. When senior leaders do handle initial interviews, they might spend a week interviewing 20 candidates but emerge with three solid prospects. These candidates then face a gauntlet of departmental interviews, where the real assessment begins. This is where you get the nuts-and-bolts questions: "I need to know you can communicate clearly because I can't read minds when deadlines are looming. I need to know you can manage time because chaos isn't a viable business strategy."

The final stage brings everyone together around a table to compare notes; think of it as a hiring version of a jury deliberation (aka as calibration). But here's the catch: raining people to conduct effective interviews is like teaching someone to ride a bike via PowerPoint. It's not just about asking questions; it's about understanding the questions behind the questions.

The key isn't finding a perfect system. It's creating a process that gives candidates room to shine while allowing the organization to properly assess them. Because at the end of the day, hiring is less like solving a math problem and more like trying to predict which way the wind will blow next Tuesday.

Getting the Role Right

This part is like building a house—you'd better have solid blueprints before breaking ground. Too many companies treat job descriptions like ancient scrolls, dusting them off only when someone quits. In an ideal world, you'd review these annually, sitting down with the current role-holder to understand what they actually do versus what some HR wizard wrote three reorganizations ago. When someone gives notice, they should be more than just a walking countdown timer to their last day. Get them involved in finding their replacement—after all, who knows the role's hidden quirks better than the person doing it?—and ask them these questions:

1. Looking back at your job description versus what you actually do, what is the biggest 'plot twist' in how this role evolved? What unexpected responsibilities or projects became central that a new person should know about?

2. What are your 'insider tips' for successfully juggling the different aspects of this role? Any unofficial systems or approaches you developed that made things run more smoothly?

3. Let's time travel to your first 90 days. Knowing what you know now, what do you wish someone had told you about this role that would have helped you get up to speed faster?

4. Everyone has different relationships with different departments. What connections or collaborations did you find most crucial for getting things done that might not be obvious from the outside?

5. If you were writing the 'unauthorized biography' of this role, what chapter would be titled 'Things Nobody Tells You but Everyone Should Know'? What are those unwritten but important aspects of the job?

How to Diagnose Your Talent Needs: The Inductive-Deductive Cycle

Before you write another job ad, run your talent challenge through this cycle to keep your process both data-driven and flexible:

Inductive Discovery

Observe *frontline realities: interview hiring managers, scan exit-interview notes, map out recurring frustrations in free-form bullet points.* **Gather** *unfiltered stories: ask "What's the one skill we're always missing?" and let the anecdotes flow.*

Hypothesis Development

Synthesize *your raw findings into 2-3 clear hypotheses (e.g., "Candidates who've led virtual teams under pressure will onboard 30% faster"). **Translate** each hypothesis into a testable question for your next interview batch.*

Deductive Testing

Design *quick validation checkpoints—mini-surveys, targeted focus groups, or A/B job-description variants—to see which hypothesis holds water.* **Measure** *against success indicators like time-to-fill, new-hire performance ratings, or 90-day retention.*

Reflect & Refine

Compare *your actual outcomes to predictions. Which traits correlated with success?* **Iterate**: *tweak your hypotheses, revise interview prompts, and loop back into the inductive phase for continuous improvement.*

This isn't rocket science; it's a research engine that keeps your hiring honest. By weaving the inductive-deductive loop into every recruitment sprint, you'll dodge generic templates and build a bespoke, always-learning talent pipeline.

The real gold comes from talking to everyone who interacts with the role. It's like conducting a 360-degree survey of a position. How do other departments engage with this role? What makes their lives easier or harder? This proactive investigation often reveals that the actual job looks about as similar to its description as a fast-food burger does to its advertisement photo.

So, when someone resigns from a position, set up "Leave Impact Interviews." This is not an exit interview (a conversation you have with the person who is exiting the organization) but an interview with people/departments who had contact/worked with the person leaving the role. To get to the heart of cognitive engagement, ask questions like these:

1. Every office has that one person who looks at a problem sideways and somehow makes magic happen. What was [departing employee]'s superpower when it came to tackling tricky challenges that affected your team?

2. We're making a 'Greatest Hits' album of [departing employee]'s best work improvements. What process or system did they put in place that would be the chart-topping single?

3. Let's play 'What's in their brain?' What unique knowledge or expertise did [departing employee] have that we should try to download before they go? Any special tricks or tips they used that made working with your department smoother?

Then there's the matter of natural attributes—those innate qualities you can't train into someone no matter how many workshops you hold. You can teach someone Excel formulas, but you can't install intellectual curiosity or integrity like downloading an app. The role needs to be structured to both require and nurture these qualities, not just list them as nice-to-haves. The hiring process itself needs to be more choreographed than a Broadway show. It's not just about checking boxes, but about creating a systematic way to evaluate whether candidates can succeed in the role. This means getting crystal clear about what success looks like: "You'll need to understand this system, manage these relationships, juggle these priorities without dropping any balls."

Having senior leadership involved early in the interview process might seem like using a sledgehammer to hang a picture, but it can save tremendous time downstream. When trained, these leaders can spot potential misfits faster than a San Franciscan spots tourists wearing shorts in June. Their questions aren't random. They're carefully crafted to reveal whether candidates have what it takes to thrive in your particular corporate ecosystem.

In the next chapter, we are going to dig into onboarding and how you can set the stage for the engagement you want to create in your organization.

The Bottom Line

The best talent often comes in unexpected packages. Build hiring systems around what actually predicts success—skills, leadership potential, and threshold attributes—and not just impressive credentials.

The Three-Bucket Hiring Framework

Skills Bucket

- Can they do the technical work required?
- Do they have the basic toolkit for the role?
- Can these skills be learned/developed if missing?

Leadership Potential Bucket

- Can they help others succeed?
- Do they demonstrate influence without authority?
- Can they navigate complex relationships and power dynamics?

Culture or Threshold Attributes Bucket (The Game-Changers)

Things you **cannot teach**:

- **Intellectual curiosity**: "Tell me about a time you challenged the status quo"
- **Integrity**: Actions match words consistently
- **Adaptability**: How they handle change and uncertainty
- **Trust-building ability**: Can they connect across different personalities?
- **Constructive challenge**: Will they push back respectfully when needed?

CHAPTER 4 MAGNETIZING TALENT: HOW TO ATTRACT THE BEST   TEAR SHEET

Immediate Actions You Can Take Today

Conduct a "Success Autopsy"

For your top performers, ask:

- What attributes do they actually share (beyond credentials)?
- How did they develop their most valuable skills?
- What questions would reveal these qualities in interviews?
- Which of their traits can't be taught?

Transform Your Job Descriptions

Stop asking: "Bachelor's degree required, 3-5 years experience"

Start asking: "What does success in this role actually look like?"

Include:

- Day-to-day realities, not just responsibilities
- Growth opportunities and challenges
- Specific threshold attributes needed
- How this role impacts the organization

Implement "Leave Impact Interviews"

When someone resigns, interview their colleagues (not just exit interview the departing person):

Questions to ask colleagues:

- "What was [departing employee]'s superpower when tackling challenges?"
- "What process improvement would be their 'chart-topping single'?"
- "What unique knowledge should we download before they go?"
- "What made working with them easier for your department?"

Questions for the departing employee:

- "What's the biggest 'plot twist' between your job description and reality?"
- "What insider tips would help your replacement succeed?"
- "What do you wish someone had told you in your first 90 days?"
- "What connections/collaborations were most crucial for getting things done?"

Red Flags in Your Current Process

Credential Obsession Warning Signs:

- All your hires come from the same schools/backgrounds
- You use alma mater as a proxy for intelligence
- "Cultural fit" means "looks/thinks like current team"
- Job descriptions read like legal documents
- Interview questions haven't changed in years

Process Problems:

- Hiring managers can't articulate what success looks like
- Same generic questions for every role
- No involvement from senior leadership until final stages
- Job descriptions copied from previous postings
- No systematic way to evaluate threshold attributes

The Doorman Principle

Remember: Excellence doesn't wear a particular pedigree. The doorman who greets residents, solves problems quickly, and communicates across social strata might have exactly the threshold attributes you need—regardless of where they went to school.

Ask yourself: Are we evaluating what people can do, or just where they've been?

Quick Diagnostic Questions

For your hiring process:

- Do our job descriptions excite qualified candidates?
- Are we asking questions that predict actual success?
- Do our "requirements" reflect what's truly necessary?
- Are we widening or narrowing our talent pool?

For candidate assessment:

- Can they do the work? (Skills)
- Can they help others succeed? (Leadership potential)
- Do they have the attributes we can't teach?
  (Threshold attributes)

Remember: The Anti-Airport Test

The "hire someone you'd want to be stuck in an airport with" metric is not a hiring strategy—it's a bias accelerator. Some of the best hires are people you might not vacation with but who are phenomenal collaborators, sharp thinkers, and generous teammates.

Focus on contribution, not comfort.

"Train people well enough so they can leave,
treat them well enough so they don't want to."
– Sir Richard Branson

CHAPTER 5

Onboard to Thrive: Setting the Stage for Engagement

Years ago, I was asked to take a look at a department with an alarming pattern: every six months, the same position became vacant. The role was well-paid, offered decent benefits, and reported to a respected director. But for some reason, people just kept leaving.

Now, I've been in HR long enough to know that when you see that kind of turnover—same role, same manager, same exit interview answers that feel . . . sanitized—you're looking at a systemic issue hiding in plain sight.

So, I started digging.

The first thing I asked to see was their onboarding plan. What I got was a glorified checklist: "Get laptop. Sign HR forms. Meet team lead. Review job description." That was it. No real training.

No context. No culture. It was onboarding as a logistical task, not a strategic moment.

Let me be clear: this wasn't a bad company. The people cared. The mission was solid. But the gap between intention and execution was massive. They were hiring smart, qualified people and then dropping them into the deep end with a PowerPoint and a prayer.

I sat down with the team and said, "Walk me through what happens on day one. And then day ten. And then day thirty."

And what I heard was . . . nothing. No real follow-up. No check-ins. No cultural integration. Just, "Well, we figured they'd ask if they needed anything."

Right.

Imagine being the new hire, eager and nervous, and your first week consists of awkward Zoom calls and a mountain of PDFs that no one explains. You don't know where the decisions happen, who the influencers are, or what people mean when they say, "We'll take it offline." It's not just confusing, it's isolating.

So, we reimagined the onboarding experience.

We started with the basics: not just what the job is, but how it connects to the larger mission. What does success look like? What are the rhythms of the team? Where can this role grow in six months or a year?

Then we layered in what I call the "two-path approach": the practical and the cultural.

Path one was about skills, systems, and processes—the nuts and bolts of the job. How do you navigate the HRIS system? Who approves budget requests? What's the protocol for requesting time off without triggering a minor drama?

Path two was deeper: how do people communicate here? Is Teams used for everything or only emergencies? Are you expected to loop in five people for every decision, or is autonomy the norm? These unwritten rules—what I sometimes call the "social operating system"—are where most new hires stumble.

We also built in some relationships on purpose. Every new hire was paired with two people: a buddy and a mentor.

The buddy was someone outside their team, there to show them the ropes. They weren't responsible for training, but they were essential in building connections. Where's the best coffee nearby? When's it okay to schedule a meeting with the VP without getting the side-eye? The buddy was their cultural GPS.

The mentor, on the other hand, played a longer game. They helped the new hire chart a path forward, learning what professional development looked like, where opportunities existed to grow, and how to navigate the power structure without stepping on landmines. One helped you feel like you belonged. The other helped you believe in where you could go.

It wasn't rocket science. It was intention. (If you want to learn more about this, get a copy of *The First 90 Days: Proven Strategies for Getting Up to Speed Faster and Smarter, Updated and Expanded,* by Michael D. Watkins on Amazon). The results were that turnover in that role dropped to zero over the next 18 months. Zero. Same hiring manager. Same job responsibilities. Different experience.

Why? Because we stopped treating onboarding like a task and started treating it like what it is: a moment of organizational imprinting. The first few weeks of a job are when people decide not just whether they can do the job, but whether they want to.

Onboarding done right sends a message: "We see you. We've thought about what you need. And we're in this with you."

Onboarding done wrong? Well, it sends a different message: "Good luck, hope you don't drown."

And no, a free water bottle and a link to the SharePoint site doesn't count as support.

One of my favorite onboarding tweaks came from a team that handed new hires a frozen yogurt gift card and told them, "Your only task this week is to use this to take someone outside your department for a 15-minute meet and greet." That tiny ritual did more for cross-functional relationships than half the org-wide meetings I've attended in my life.

So, if you're still thinking onboarding is a one-week orientation with some swag and a system tutorial, let me stop you right here.

Onboarding is culture in action.

It's how you teach the rhythm, not just the rules. It's how you show what you value, not just what you measure. And it's your best shot at turning a new hire into a long-term contributor.

Because when people feel grounded, connected, and clear about what's expected of them, they stay.

They thrive.

And no one gets surprised when, six months in, they haven't magically learned the difference between "optional" meetings and *actually* optional meetings.

That success story wasn't a one-off, it was a turning point. It showed us that onboarding isn't just about checklists or compliance. It's about culture, clarity, and connection. And when we get it right, it lays the groundwork for every other piece of the engagement puzzle.

So now that we've seen what's possible, let's zoom out and look at what really makes onboarding work— not just for one team, but across an entire organization.

• • •

In the previous chapter, we explored how different types of engagement, particularly cognitive engagement, are shaped by organizational infrastructure—everything from process design to role clarity. Think of it as the foundation of your workplace home. When these elements align properly, they create an environment where employees can thrive and contribute their best work.

So, you may ask, how do we set up the new hire and the organization for a successful life together? Great question! In the HR world, we call that Onboarding, but it may not be what you think it is.

The Evolution of Onboarding

Onboarding is that critical period after successfully attracting talent to your organization. This isn't just about paperwork and passwords (though those matter too). It's about helping new hires understand both the written and unwritten rules of their new professional home. Good onboarding connects individuals to your organizational culture, teaches them how to navigate social norms, and sets them up for success both personally and professionally.

An effective onboarding program operates along two essential paths:

The first path focuses on skills, processes, and tasks—the "how-to" manual of getting things done in your organization. For example, if you're bringing on an HR professional, they need to learn the nuts and bolts: How do they administer benefits? What's the protocol for handling employee relations issues? Which HRIS systems do they use, and how do these systems handle everything from payroll to promotions? This technical knowledge forms the backbone of their ability to perform effectively.

The second path, equally crucial but often overlooked, is cultural integration. This is where new hires learn to read between the lines of your employee handbook. They discover how your organization really operates: Is communication primarily through email or do people prefer impromptu Zoom huddles? Are in-person lunches the norm for relationship building? Do people typically collaborate across departments, or does each team operate more independently? These cultural elements might seem subtle, but they're fundamental to success. This cultural piece includes understanding what some might call "office politics," though I prefer to think of it as organizational dynamics. It's about learning the informal networks and relationships that help get things done.

Who are the go-to people for specific challenges? How do decisions get made, and when should you schedule meetings versus having quick corridor conversations? These unwritten rules can be either positive forces that facilitate collaboration and efficiency, or negative influences that create barriers; it all depends on how they're shaped and communicated during onboarding.

Effective onboarding isn't about overwhelming new hires with information. It's about creating a structured journey that helps them master both the technical and cultural aspects of their new environment. When done right, it accelerates their path to productivity while fostering genuine engagement with their work and colleagues.

Building the Two-Pronged Approach

A successful onboarding program must address several fundamental questions for new employees. First and foremost: "What does this organization truly believe in?" This goes beyond the mission statement framed in the lobby. Whether you're a nonprofit focused on social change or a tech company developing the next innovation, every organization needs to communicate its purpose with clarity. New hires should understand not just what you do, but why you do it. Let's put this in the context of the employee lifecycle.

Think of employment as a journey with distinct phases. It starts with attracting and acquiring talent (which we covered earlier), moves into onboarding, continues through development, management, and retention (we'll dive into those soon), and concludes with offboarding. Each phase serves a specific purpose in creating engaged, productive employees.

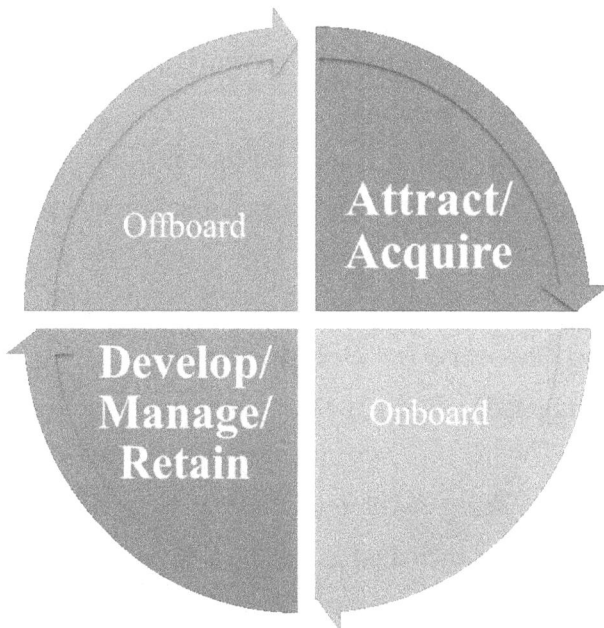

Historically, onboarding focused primarily on compliance—making sure all the bureaucratic boxes were checked. You know the drill: I-9 forms, W-2s, direct deposit authorizations, and the mountain of paperwork required by various government agencies. While these administrative tasks remain necessary for record-keeping and legal compliance, modern onboarding has evolved into something far more meaningful.

Today's onboarding represents a dynamic exchange between employer and employee. It's about establishing a symbiotic relationship where both parties understand their roles in contributing to each other's success. Organizations invest in properly integrating new hires into their culture and systems, while employees bring their unique perspectives and skills to enhance the workplace. This mutual investment sets the stage for long-term engagement and productivity. Modern organizations recognize that proper onboarding is an investment that pays dividends in employee satisfaction, retention, and performance. When new hires clearly understand both their practical responsibilities and their place in the larger organizational ecosystem, they're better equipped to contribute meaningfully from day one, and the process definitely takes longer than one day or one week.

Creating Meaningful Connections

Today's progressive organizations are transforming onboarding from a checklist into an immersive experience. Take Riverbed Technologies, where new hires participate in "A Day in the Life" simulations during their first week. Instead of just reading about company processes, they work through realistic scenarios with experienced team members. This hands-on approach helps them understand not just what to do, but why certain processes exist.

Digital innovation has also revolutionized onboarding. Companies are moving beyond basic training videos to create interactive learning experiences. Picture a new manager at Metro Health accessing a digital platform that combines essential training modules with real-time connection to mentors. They complete required compliance training but also engage in virtual coffee chats with team members across different departments, getting authentic insights into company culture.

Here are some practical approaches that work:

- Organizations are implementing several effective approaches to enhance their onboarding experience. A structured buddy system serves as a cornerstone, pairing new hires with experienced employees outside their immediate team to foster cross-departmental relationships from the very beginning. Regular culture conversations bring small groups of new hires together with senior leaders to discuss and understand organizational values in action.

- Project-based onboarding takes this a step further by engaging new employees in actual business challenges within their first month, allowing them to apply their skills while learning company processes. To ensure continuous support and feedback, organizations implement regular check-in sessions throughout the first 90 days, moving beyond the traditional first-week-only approach. Where appropriate, department rotation programs give new hires exposure to different aspects of the business, broadening their organizational perspective.

The key is creating touchpoints that go beyond the traditional "Here's your desk, here's your computer" approach. When organizations invest this kind of thought into onboarding, they see tangible results: faster productivity, stronger team connections, and higher retention rates.

Understanding Stakeholder Relationships

Let's talk about the exchange between organizations and employees; it's more nuanced than just trading time for money. When new employees join, they need to understand both the explicit and implicit rewards of good performance. Yes, there's the paycheck—that's fundamental. But successful organizations offer a broader value proposition: opportunities for professional development, access to leadership, enhanced benefits, and paths for advancement. By clearly communicating these opportunities during onboarding (and beyond), organizations effectively teach new hires what success looks like and how to achieve it.

We can break down the critical questions every onboarding program needs to address, starting with the tactical side. The fundamental question is: "What's my role, and how does it contribute to our collective success?" New hires need to understand how their individual efforts connect to departmental goals and ultimately support organizational objectives. Think of it as helping them see their piece of the puzzle and how it fits into the bigger picture.

Equally important is understanding their network of support and influence. New employees need clarity about three key groups:

1. The foundation of success begins with a strong direct support network. This critical group includes immediate supervisors, mentors, and experienced colleagues who provide guidance, feedback, and problem-solving help with daily challenges.

2. Beyond this immediate circle lies the Internal Stakeholder network. For instance, HR professionals must understand their service extends to the entire organization, from entry-level employees to senior leadership, as their decisions and actions impact everyone's workplace experience.

3. External Stakeholders form the third vital group, encompassing potential recruits, vendors, clients, and community partners. Understanding these relationships helps employees grasp the full scope of their responsibilities.

This stakeholder mapping isn't just an academic exercise; it's the key to success. When employees understand their support system and spheres of influence, they make better decisions and build stronger professional relationships. For instance, a marketing manager needs to know not just their team's goals, but how their work affects sales targets, customer experience, and brand reputation.

A well-designed onboarding program weaves all these elements together. It helps new hires understand both their concrete responsibilities and their place in the organization's ecosystem. This comprehensive understanding accelerates their path to productivity and increases their likelihood of long-term success and engagement.

At Microsoft, they get fancy with their "One Week" program. Instead of spending their first days pretending to remember 47 new names, engineers create detailed maps of who's who in their corporate zoo, from the coffee machine expert to that one person who mysteriously knows everyone's birthday. They're forced to have actual human conversations (the horror!) through "connection sessions" where they learn the unwritten rules, like never touching Dave's labeled yogurt in the break room. By the end of the week, they've not only figured out how their code fits into Microsoft's master plan, but also which Teams channels have the best memes. This investment in thorough onboarding pays dividends in faster employee integration and higher engagement levels.

Critical questions that shape an employee's success are "threshold attributes." New hires need to understand what excellence looks like in your organization. What are those fundamental characteristics that set high performers apart? Maybe it's intellectual curiosity, or perhaps it's the ability to navigate ambiguity with grace. When I worked with an asset management company, they made sure that during onboarding, new employees knew what these attributes were, what they looked like for their particular job, and how they integrated into all aspects of their work. This was made explicit by sharing stories of successful employees—not just their achievements, but the behaviors and mindsets that got them there.

Next comes the nuts and bolts of role expectations. This goes beyond a simple job description. Employees need crystal clarity about their responsibilities, required skills, and performance metrics. Think of the difference between telling a new financial analyst, "You'll handle accounts payable," versus providing them with a comprehensive understanding of payment cycles, vendor relationships, and how their work impacts cash flow. One sets them up for basic competence; the other prepares them for excellence.

Every organization has its own operational DNA. A new finance team member needs to understand not just how to process payroll, but how their role interconnects with other departments. How does their work affect HR's ability to make offers? How do their reports influence strategic planning? This understanding transforms routine tasks into meaningful contributions.

Now, here's something that often gets overlooked but can make or break someone's success: communication norms. I once consulted for a company where crucial decisions happened during impromptu hallway conversations, but nobody told that to new hires. They kept waiting for formal meetings that never came.

Organizations need to be explicit about their communication culture: Is it email-first or walk-in-friendly? Do people expect immediate responses, or is it okay to batch communications? Are Teams messages acceptable for urgent issues, or is that a phone call scenario? These unwritten rules often determine success as much as technical skills do. Here's what makes these questions so powerful: they address both the explicit and implicit aspects of organizational life. It's not enough to tell someone how to do their job; they need to understand how to navigate the organization's social and operational landscape.

An organization that does this right is the consulting firm

McKinsey & Company. During the first two weeks, new consultants are introduced to what they playfully call "The McKinsey Way of War Room Communications" (though I'm sure they have a more corporate-friendly name for it now). They learn that different communication channels serve distinct purposes: Teams chat is for quick alignment and informal brainstorming, email is for formal client communications and deliverable sharing, and "walk-ins" to partner offices (or virtual drop-ins) are not just acceptable but encouraged for time-sensitive decisions.

New hires participate in simulation exercises where they handle realistic scenarios, like a client suddenly changing the project scope at 7 p.m. or a partner requesting analysis with unclear parameters. These exercises help them internalize when to escalate issues, whom to loop in, and most importantly, through which channel. This kind of clarity accelerates integration and reduces anxiety for new team members.

The Power of Dual Support: Buddies and Mentors

We've already touched on how relationships shape engagement, but it's worth circling back to clear up a common confusion: buddies and mentors are not the same thing. Think of them as playing different roles in the workplace ecosystem—both vital, but very different species. I've seen this play out across multiple organizations, and once we stopped treating them as interchangeable, the results spoke for themselves.

A mentor helps you grow your career. A buddy helps you survive your first week without accidentally CC'ing the entire company. At one consulting firm, we paired new hires with buddies from other departments—folks with just enough experience to know where the bodies were buried but not so much seniority that they'd already forgotten what it was like to be new. These buddies weren't coaching on career goals, but were dishing out the real intel: which meetings are secretly optional, where to find the good snacks, and why one VP always speaks in sports metaphors no one understands.

Your buddy is the person who tells you that while the dress code says, "business casual," people actually wear jeans on Thursdays. They explain why the marketing team prefers morning meetings and why you should always bring data to conversations with the analytics group. They're not teaching you how to do your job. They're teaching you how to belong.

Mentors play a different but equally crucial role. They are your professional development champions, typically more senior colleagues who help chart your career path within the organization. A mentor helps you see the bigger picture: where your skills could take you, which projects might advance your career, and how to navigate professional challenges.

Here's why this two-pronged approach matters. Buddies focus on immediate acclimatization and cultural fit; they serve multiple essential functions in the onboarding process. They create an environment where new employees feel comfortable and connected to the organization. These cultural guides explain the unwritten rules and customs that shape daily work life while providing a safe space for asking those questions that might seem too basic or obvious. Perhaps most importantly, they help new hires build their initial network, laying the groundwork for long-term organizational relationships.

Mentors concentrate on developing long-term professional trajectories. They take an active role in helping develop career strategies and serve as advocates for advancement opportunities. Through their experience, they provide valuable industry and organizational insights that go beyond day-to-day operations. Additionally, they connect mentees to higher-level opportunities, opening doors that might otherwise remain closed.

The timing of these relationships is crucial. A buddy becomes essential from day one; they're your lifeline during those first few months when everything feels new and potentially overwhelming. A mentor relationship often develops more gradually, becoming more valuable as you settle into your role and start thinking about growth opportunities. Many times, these mentor relationships happen organically and can be facilitated by leaders within the organization.

This dual support system has two critical outcomes. First, it establishes Psychological Safety, a type of environment created by Amy Edmonson where having trusted guides helps new hires feel secure enough to ask questions and take appropriate risks. Second, it builds Strong Connections and creates relationships that form the foundation for lasting organizational networks.

Here's what makes mentorship fundamentally different from other forms of organizational support:

It's focused on long-term professional growth rather than immediate acclimation. It provides strategic career guidance beyond day-to-day job performance. It offers insights into organizational dynamics that aren't written in any manual. Additionally, it creates advocacy opportunities at higher levels of the organization.

Integrating the Engagement Trifecta

Now, here's where everything comes together beautifully in a well-designed onboarding program. We're creating bridges between different types of engagement:

- *Cognitive Engagement (aka "I think")* manifests through several key elements. It begins with a thorough understanding of job requirements and progressively builds through mastery of necessary skills. This type of engagement deepens as employees learn organizational processes and continue developing their professional competencies.

- *Affective Engagement (aka "I feel")* centers on the emotional connections within the workplace. It involves developing genuine organizational commitment and finding personal meaning in one's work. Through this dimension, employees create a sense of workplace belonging that goes beyond mere job satisfaction.

- *Social Engagement* (aka "I belong") focuses on building the interpersonal framework necessary for success. This includes forming professional relationships and developing a deep understanding of cultural norms. Through this engagement, employees build robust support networks and create collaborative partnerships that enhance their effectiveness within the organization.

When these three elements align through effective onboarding, something remarkable happens. You get employees who aren't just competent at their jobs but are genuinely connected to their work and their colleagues. They understand not just what they need to do, but why it matters and how it fits into the bigger picture. This comprehensive approach to onboarding creates what I call the "engagement trifecta"—people who think well, feel good, and connect meaningfully with their work environment.

Inclusive leadership transforms how we think about the relationship between leaders and their teams. It's not just about having diverse faces in the room - it's about actively seeking out, valuing, and incorporating different perspectives into every discussion and decision. When I work with organizations to develop inclusive leaders, I emphasize that their role goes beyond traditional management. They must actively advocate for their team members' diverse needs and values. This isn't just feel-good corporate speak; it's about creating tangible results through better decision-making and innovation.

Think about the shift this represents: We're moving from viewing diversity as a legal checkbox to recognizing it as a fundamental driver of organizational success. What makes this approach powerful is how it reframes our thinking about workplace equality. Instead of focusing on meeting demographic targets, inclusive leadership tackles the root causes of exclusion and marginalization. It's about developing specific skills in relationship building, collaboration, and creating truly inclusive spaces where everyone can contribute meaningfully.

The real magic happens when leaders master these competencies, from building partnerships to achieving genuine consensus. They create workplaces where engagement isn't just a buzzword but a daily reality.

You probably already understand that this is about relationships between leaders and followers. Leaders may adopt different relationship approaches: adaptive relationships that emphasize collaboration to find solutions, or boundary-spanning relationships where leaders acknowledge individual uniqueness while guiding teams toward shared goals. Regardless of the approach, these relationships must honor the human need for connection and community, with the dynamic held between the leader and the individual or team.

When Trust Breaks: The Push for Broader Leadership

The business world has changed dramatically in recent decades, and leaders have had to adapt their approach accordingly. Gone are the days when CEOs could focus solely on their employees and shareholders while ignoring everyone else. The stark reality is that corporate mishaps and scandals have eroded public trust, from environmental disasters to accounting fraud to workplace harassment. These failures forced organizations to take a hard look in the mirror and realize they needed to think bigger about their responsibilities.

Think about it: When an oil tanker runs aground and destroys an ecosystem, or when executives cook the books to inflate profits, or when workplace harassment goes unchecked, it doesn't just affect the company's bottom line. It impacts communities, damages the environment, and breaks public trust. These wake-up calls pushed leaders to expand their vision of who they are accountable to.

Today's leaders must consider a whole ecosystem of stakeholders: their employees (of course), but also their customers, business partners, the communities they operate in, and even the environment itself. It's like conducting an orchestra; you need to pay attention to all the instruments to create harmony, not just focus on the violins.

This shift led organizations to grapple with two fundamental questions. First, "What are we really here for?" It's not just about making money anymore, though that's certainly important. Companies need to define what success looks like in a way that considers all their stakeholders. The second question is trickier: "What do we owe these stakeholders?" This is where the rubber meets the road. Leaders must figure out how to balance competing interests while staying true to their values and maintaining sustainable business practices.

These aren't just philosophical questions; they're practical challenges that shape how modern organizations operate. Leaders today need to be like bridge builders, creating connections between different stakeholder groups while maintaining a clear vision of where they're heading. It's about finding ways to do business that are not just profitable but also just, sustainable, and accountable to everyone involved.

These two fundamental questions about purpose and responsibility have pushed organizations to rethink what leadership really means in today's world. It's no longer enough to just focus on what happens inside your company's walls. Modern leaders need to balance both internal and external responsibilities, like a tightrope walker keeping their eye on both ends of the wire.

Some experts call this "responsible inclusive leadership," which sounds like a fancy term, I know, but stick with me here. Think of it as leadership that looks both inward and outward. On the inside, it's about creating an inclusive workplace where everyone can thrive. On the outside, it's about considering your organization's impact on the broader world. This approach is miles away from the old-school "born leader" mentality that focused on individual traits. Instead, it's all about building relationships and understanding how everything connects.

This shift in thinking isn't new. It dates back to the 1950s when a scholar named Howard Bowen laid out three basic responsibilities for businesses. First, run your business well enough to create jobs and drive economic growth (pretty straightforward, right?) Second, treat your employees and customers fairly and honestly (seems obvious, but you'd be surprised how often this gets overlooked). And third, actively work to improve your community and environment (because success isn't just about the bottom line).

Later, other thinkers built on this foundation and made it more practical. They suggested companies need three key elements to make this work: clear ethical principles (your moral compass), formal processes (your game plan), and specific policies (your rulebook). It's like building a house: you need a solid foundation (your principles), a good blueprint (your processes), and clear instructions (your policies) to make it all come together.

This foundation for corporate responsibility didn't stay static; it kept evolving. In the early 1990s, researchers started looking beyond just having good intentions and nice-sounding policies. They began asking the tough questions: What actual impact are we having? How do we measure success? It was like switching from grading on effort to grading on results.

Around this time, a game-changing idea emerged called the Triple Bottom Line, or as some like to call it, the three Ps: Profit, People, and Planet. It's a simple but powerful concept: Companies shouldn't just measure their success by how much money they make (Profit), but also by how they treat people (People) and what impact they have on the environment (Planet). Think of it as a three-legged stool. If any leg is weak, the whole thing becomes unstable.

This approach pushed companies to work together in ways they never had before. After all, no single organization can solve climate change or eliminate poverty on its own. It's like a potluck dinner— everyone brings something to the table, and together you create something better than anyone could have made alone.

. . .

The implications of stakeholder responsibility and accountability run deep through day-to-day operations. Leaders need to clearly communicate their organization's goals and values to everyone involved. It's not enough to have fancy mission statements framed on the wall; these ideas need to translate into specific, measurable goals that every employee can understand and work toward.

When employees can see how their work connects to the bigger picture, magic happens. Research shows that people perform better when they understand how their individual goals tie into the organization's broader strategy. It's like being part of a massive jigsaw puzzle—when you can see where your piece fits, you're more motivated to make it work.

This connection between individual contributions and organizational success is absolutely crucial for creating an inclusive culture. When leaders can get everyone thinking about how they contribute to the bigger picture, it creates what one expert calls a "collective alignment," where everything from strategy to systems to staff skills all point in the same direction. It's like getting an entire orchestra to play in perfect harmony—not easy, but when it works, the results are spectacular.

This raises an important question: if goal setting acts as a compass for employees, helping them align their work with organizational objectives, does it also affect how they connect with and engage with their workplace? The research is clear on this: it absolutely does.

When organizations implement thoughtful goal-setting practices, they create a positive feedback loop. Employees develop stronger relationships with their organization because they understand their role in its success. They focus their energy on activities that matter, become more motivated to excel, and generally feel more optimistic about their work and future opportunities.

Companies that take this seriously, whether they're driven by regulatory compliance, strategic advantages, or deeply held values, create an environment where employees can thrive. By actively engaging their workforce in meaningful goal setting, these organizations lay the groundwork for sustained employee engagement. It's a straightforward principle with profound implications: When people understand where they're going and why it matters, they're more likely to invest themselves fully in the journey.

The relationship between leaders and their organizations has undergone a fundamental transformation. As markets became more global and interconnected, the old model of top-down leadership started showing its cracks. Leaders discovered that success required more than just managing their immediate sphere of influence; it meant understanding and responding to an intricate web of relationships that extends far beyond office walls.

This shift wasn't voluntary. A string of corporate failures and scandals over the past few decades exposed the limitations of narrow leadership approaches. Major environmental disasters destroyed ecosystems, financial frauds wiped out life savings, and workplace misconduct damaged countless lives. Each crisis demonstrated how the actions of leaders could ripple outward, affecting not just employees and shareholders but entire communities, environments, and future generations.

Modern leaders now need to consider a much broader group of stakeholders. Sure, we're talking about employees, but also clients, customers, business partners, the environment, and shareholders. It's about rebuilding public trust and maintaining what I call your "license to operate" in society. As one of my mentors used to say, it's about making profits with principles.

This evolution raises two fundamental questions every organization needs to answer:

What's our real purpose as a company?

What do we owe our stakeholders?

These aren't just philosophical musings. They're practical questions that help define success metrics and guide business practices. This is where "responsible inclusive leadership" comes in—a concept that balances both internal organizational needs and external responsibilities while focusing on ethical and sustainable practices.

Let's look at how this plays out in Corporate Social Responsibility (CSR). Again, Howard Bowen laid the groundwork back in 1953 with three basic responsibilities:

- Run successful businesses that create jobs and drive economic growth

- Operate fairly and honestly

- Actively improve community and environmental conditions

This framework has evolved over time, becoming more sophisticated and actionable. Today's successful organizations understand that their impact goes beyond profit margins; they need to consider their effect on people and the planet (the Triple Bottom Line).

The beauty of this approach? When organizations clearly communicate these broader goals and values, employees can connect their individual work to the bigger picture. This alignment doesn't just sound good; research shows it leads to higher performance and stronger engagement. It's about creating what I call "collective alignment," where strategy, structure, systems, and skills all work together toward shared goals.

The Bottom Line

Onboarding is culture in action—not just a checklist, but organizational imprinting. The first few weeks determine whether people decide they can do the job AND whether they want to. Poor onboarding creates turnover; great onboarding creates engagement from day one.

The Two-Path Onboarding Framework

Path One: Technical Integration

Skills, systems, and processes—the "how-to" manual:

- Master essential tools and systems
- Understand role responsibilities and performance metrics
- Learn organizational processes and workflows
- Connect individual tasks to broader objectives
- Clarify escalation procedures and decision-making authority

Path Two: Cultural Integration

- The "social operating system" and unwritten rules:
- Understand communication norms and channels
- Learn organizational dynamics and informal networks
- Grasp decision-making culture and meeting rhythms
- Build relationships across departments
- Navigate organizational values in practice

Immediate Actions You Can Take Today

Audit Your Current Onboarding

Ask these critical questions:

- What happens on day 1, day 10, day 30, day 60, and beyond?
- Do new hires understand both their job AND how it connects to the mission?
- Do people know the difference between "optional" and actually optional meetings?
- Are we creating connections or just giving information?

Implement the Dual Support System

Buddy System (Cultural GPS):

- Pair new hires with someone OUTSIDE their immediate team
- Focus on cultural navigation, not job training
- Buddy answers: "Where's the best coffee? When can you interrupt the VP? What does 'take it offline' really mean?"
- Duration: First 3-6 months

Mentor System (Career Champion):

- Match with more senior colleague for long-term development
- Focus on career trajectory and professional growth
- Mentor provides: strategic guidance, organizational insights, advocacy opportunities
- Duration: 6-12 months minimum

Address the Five Critical Onboarding Questions

1. "What does this organization truly believe in?"

- Go beyond mission statements to lived values and what they look like
- Share specific stories of organizational principles in action
- Connect daily work to larger purpose

2. "What does success look like here?"

- Define threshold attributes for high performers
- Share concrete examples and behavioral indicators
- Clarify both short-term and long-term expectations

3. "How do things really get done?"

- Map decision-making processes and approval chains
- Explain communication preferences and channels
- Identify key influencers and go-to people

4. "Who's in my network?"

- **Direct Support**: Immediate supervisors, mentors, experienced colleagues
- **Internal Stakeholders**: Everyone the role serves within the organization
- **External Stakeholders**: Clients, vendors, community partners, recruits

5. "How do I navigate the unwritten rules?"

- Timing for different types of meetings and communications
- Appropriate channels for various message types
- Cultural norms around collaboration and autonomy

Innovative Onboarding Techniques

"Day in the Life" Simulations:

- Work through realistic scenarios with experienced team members

- Practice decision making in safe environment
- Learn not just what to do, but why processes exist

Connection Challenges:

- Give new hires a frozen yogurt/coffee gift card to take someone from another department for 15-minute meet-and-greet
- Create scavenger hunts that require cross-departmental interactions
- Assign cultural exploration tasks that build relationships

Project-Based Integration:

- Engage new hires in actual business challenges within first month
- Allow them to apply skills while learning company processes
- Create immediate sense of contribution and value

Engagement Trifecta Integration

Cognitive Engagement ("I Think")

- Clear understanding of job requirements and success metrics
- Mastery of necessary skills and organizational processes
- Connection between individual tasks and company objectives
- Ongoing professional development opportunities

Affective Engagement ("I Feel")

- Emotional connection to organizational mission and values
- Sense of personal meaning in daily work
- Positive feelings about contribution and impact
- Recognition and appreciation for efforts

Social Engagement ("I Belong")

- Strong professional relationships across the organization
- Understanding of cultural norms and expectations
- Robust support networks and collaborative partnerships
- Sense of inclusion and psychological safety

Warning Signs Your Onboarding is Failing

Process Red Flags:

- High turnover in same roles repeatedly
- New hires asking basic questions months later
- Lack of cross-departmental relationships
- Extended time to productivity
- Exit interviews citing confusion about expectations

Cultural Red Flags:

- New hires seem isolated or disconnected
- Frequent miscommunications about priorities
- Inability to navigate organizational dynamics
- Lack of engagement in team activities
- Quick resignation after initial enthusiasm

Manager Development for Onboarding Success

Critical Manager Skills:

- **Inclusive Communication**: Adapt style to individual team member preferences
- **Cultural Translation**: Explain "how we do things here" explicitly

- **Connection Facilitation**: Help new hires build relationships beyond immediate team
- **Goal Alignment**: Connect individual work to organizational purpose
- **Continuous Support**: Provide ongoing feedback and development opportunities

Measuring Onboarding Success

Track These Metrics:

- **Time to productivity**: How quickly new hires reach expected performance levels
- **90-day retention**: Percentage staying beyond initial adjustment period
- **Relationship indicators**: Cross-departmental connections and collaborative partnerships
- **Engagement scores**: Early indicators of "I think," "I feel," and "I belong"

Diagnostic Questions for New Hires:

- "Do you understand how your work connects to our larger mission?"
- "Can you identify at least three people outside your team you could go to for help?"
- "Do you feel comfortable asking questions and admitting what you don't know?"
- "Are you clear on what success looks like in your first 90 days?"

The Stakeholder Connection

Help new hires understand their impact on:

- **Internal stakeholders**: How their work affects colleagues and other departments
- **External stakeholders**: Clients, community, environment, shareholders
- **Future stakeholders**: Long-term organizational sustainability and growth
- **Key message**: "Your individual goals are connected to our collective success, and our success serves a purpose bigger than profit."

Remember: Onboarding Never Really Ends

Great onboarding isn't a one-week orientation—it's a gradual integration that can take 6-12 months. The goal is to turn new hires into long-term contributors who feel grounded, connected, and clear about expectations.

Bottom line: When people feel seen, supported, and connected to purpose from day one, they don't just stay—they thrive.

*"If we win the hearts and minds of employees,
we're going to have better business success."*
– Mary Barra

CHAPTER 6

Developing, Managing & Retaining Talent

Hoping that managers naturally know how to grow and retain talent is like hoping your teenager will remember to take the trash out without being asked. You can hope. But you'd better have a backup plan.

At one company I worked with we would go through our performance evaluation process every year and I'd meet with each senior manager one-on-one to review their team. Not just for ratings. For real development conversations. And we used one of my favorite tools to do it: the 9-Box Grid.

Now, if you're in HR, you've probably used the 9-Box. And if you haven't? Well, it's time. (Note: I recognize the that 9-Box is as polarizing as pineapple on pizza, so I invite you to make your own decision by reading *Think Outside the 9 Box – TalentQ* or *Humpty*

Dumpty and the 9-Box: Five Steps to Putting it Back Together Again Using the Science of Leadership Potential).

The grid is simple: three levels of performance on one axis, and three levels of potential on the other. You get nine boxes that help you sort your people into categories like "Consistent Star," "Emerging Leader," or (my personal favorite) "Solid Performer, Limited Potential," which sounds meaner than it is, but hey, clarity is kindness.

• • •

Here's how it worked. I'd sit down with each senior manager, and we'd talk through their team member by member.

"Okay," I'd say, "let's talk about Maya. Where would you place her on the grid?"

"Well, she's solid," the manager might say. "Her performance is steady. She's dependable."

"And her potential?" I'd ask.

Long pause.

This is where things always got interesting.

Because what often came out was that the manager hadn't thought much about Maya's future. Or if they had, it was vague— maybe, someday, she could lead something. But nothing was in motion.

That's the beauty of the 9-Box. It forces a conversation not just about 'how people are doing,' but 'where they're going.' Are they coasting? Stuck? Ready to stretch? Do they need a push, a mentor, a new challenge? Or, let's be honest, some direct feedback?

These weren't just HR exercises. They were leadership tests. Could a manager articulate what made someone successful? Could they name what was missing? Could they offer a plan?

And when they couldn't—which happened more often than you'd think—it told me everything I needed to know about their readiness to lead.

But here's the thing: most of these managers weren't incompetent. They were untrained. No one had taught them how to coach, how to develop people, how to hold a growth conversation without either sugarcoating or steamrolling. They were promoted based on their technical expertise, not because they knew how to build high-performing, engaged teams.

So, we started changing that. After each 9-Box session, I worked with managers to script and structure development conversations.

Let's say you had someone in the "High Potential, Inconsistent Performer" box. That's the category that gives most managers a headache. It's the person who shows flashes of brilliance . . . and then misses a key deadline. What do you do?

We'd role-play.

"Okay," I'd say. "You're talking to James. How do you open?"

They'd say something like, "James, you're smart, but sometimes you drop the ball."

"Nope," I'd say. "Try again."

Eventually, we'd get to something like:

"James, I see you as someone with real leadership potential. Your ideas are sharp, and your ability to connect dots across teams is a strength. But to move forward, we need to see more consistency in execution. I want to help you get there."

That's development. Honest, supportive, actionable.

We'd also have the other conversation, the one everyone avoids: the "Solid Performer, Low Potential" talk. Because not everyone wants to lead. And that's okay. But it's not okay to pretend otherwise.

"Anita, you are someone I trust to get the job done. You've built real credibility in this role. If you're happy here, I want to make sure you have what you need to keep thriving. And if you want something different, we can explore that too."

No shame. No condescension. Just clarity.

Development Conversations That Miss the Mark:

X Bad Example (Vague & Deflating)

"You're doing fine. Keep it up. I'll let you know if anything opens up."

Why it fails: Offers no feedback, no growth path, and no sense that the manager actually sees the employee.

Development Conversations That Build Trust & Momentum

Good Example (Clear & Empowering)

"You've taken real ownership of the X project, and your ability to bring the team together didn't go unnoticed. If you're interested in growing into a team lead role, let's talk through what skills you want to develop over the next six months and how I can support that."

Why it works: Gives specific recognition, signals future potential, and invites two-way planning and support.

And here's the part no one tells you: When you treat people like adults and speak openly about their trajectory, they don't run away. They stay. Because they trust you. Because you're not selling them empty promises. You're building something with them.

One year after our 9-Box reviews, a manager came back to me and said, "Roz, I had the best one-on-one I've ever had with my team member. She said no one had ever asked her where she wanted to grow."

No one had asked. That stuck with me.

Developing and retaining talent isn't just about pay bumps or training budgets. It's about 'attention.' Managers who are too busy to check in, who only give feedback once a year, and who treat development like a checkbox? They're the reason people leave.

And I'll say this bluntly: if your managers don't know how to have these conversations, they shouldn't be managers yet. Period.

We have to stop assuming that management is an automatic next step. It's not a reward. It's a responsibility.

And part of that responsibility is knowing your people—not just what they do but what they're capable of. Not just their output but their potential.

That's what the 9-Box helps reveal. That's why I used it every year. Because without it, we'd default to what we 'think' we know. The loudest person in the room gets promoted. The quiet high performer gets overlooked. The one who plays golf with the VP gets the raise. And the rest of your team? They start looking elsewhere.

Talent development isn't magic. But it does take intention. Structure. And time.

Time to talk.

Time to ask questions.

Time to map out a path.

And yes, time to have hard conversations.

But you know what takes *more* time? Reposting the same job six months later. Explaining to a client why their favorite analyst quit. Losing institutional knowledge because no one thought to ask what that person needed to stay.

This chapter is about how we stop that cycle. It's about building systems that work—ones that help managers show up better, help employees grow, and help organizations keep the people who make them great.

Because in the end, talent doesn't just need to be managed. It needs to be *seen*.

	Low Potential	Moderate Potential	High Potential
Low Perf.	Misaligned Role	Inconsistent Contrib.	High Risk, High Upside
Moderate Perf.	Steady Contributor	Solid Performer	Emerging Leader
High Perf.	Valued Specialist	Growth Candidate	Future Star

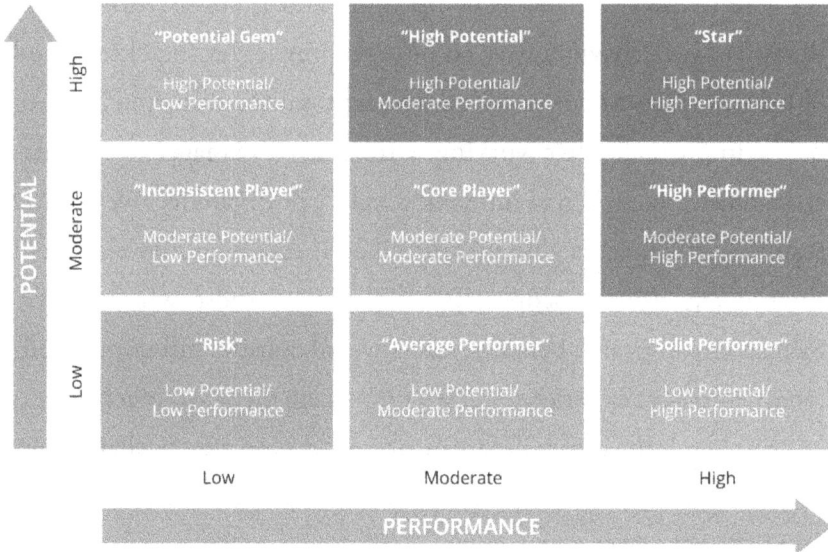

Use this framework to identify not just how employees are performing, but how they might grow. Every box calls for a different kind of leadership.

The Manager's Role in Employee Engagement

Let's dive into what I consider the real engine room of organizational success—the critical phase where managers shape employee experience day in and day out. We're talking about the "maintain, develop, and retain" stage of the employee lifecycle, and believe me, this is where the rubber meets the road in creating an engaged workforce.

Think about it: Managers are the ones who translate your organization's grand vision into daily reality. They're the ones who either nurture or inadvertently squash employee engagement. I've seen brilliant company cultures crumble because managers weren't equipped to sustain them, and I've watched struggling teams transform when managers got this piece right.

The research on this is compelling, and it consistently shows that manager behaviors have an outsized impact on the "I feel" and "I belong" parts of employee engagement, satisfaction, and sense of belonging. I remember working with an asset manager to measure engagement scores across different teams. The differences were stark; teams with managers who prioritized connection and development showed engagement scores 40% higher than those who didn't.[17] Same company, same benefits, same overall culture, but entirely different employee experiences based on management approach.

But here's the thing: before organizations can effectively support their managers in creating these positive environments, they need to take a hard look at two fundamental elements. First, they need to develop a crystal-clear understanding of their current culture—not

---

17 Harter, J. K., Schmidt, F. L., & Hayes, T. L. (2002). Business-unit-level relationship between employee satisfaction, employee engagement, and business outcomes: A meta-analysis. Journal of Applied Psychology, 87(2), 268-279.

just the values painted on the wall, but how things really work on the ground. Second, and perhaps more critically, they need to assess how inclusive that culture truly is. Are all voices being heard? Do people feel safe bringing their whole selves to work?

Understanding and Assessing Organizational Culture

Understanding your organizational culture isn't like checking the temperature; it's more like getting a full medical workup. You need to look at multiple indicators and listen to various voices. When I work with companies on this, I always start by asking employees at all levels three simple but revealing questions: "What behaviors get rewarded here?" "What and how do people tell their success stories?" and "What unwritten rules do new employees need to learn?"

The answers often surprise leadership. I remember working with a financial services firm that prided itself on innovation, yet their employees consistently reported that following established procedures was the surest path to recognition and advancement. This kind of disconnect between stated values and lived experience creates what I call the "culture credibility gap."

Now, let's talk about those management practices that research shows move the needle on engagement. It's not about grand gestures or fancy programs. It's about consistent, intentional behaviors that make people feel valued and supported. Think of it as the difference between a crash diet and developing healthy eating habits. One might show quick results, but the other creates lasting change.

Effective Management Practices that Drive Engagement

I've observed time and again that the most effective managers focus on what I call the "daily drumbeat" of engagement. These aren't dramatic interventions or complex programs; they're consistent practices that build trust, respect, and connection over time. Let me share what I've seen work across industries, backed by solid research.

First, there's the power of regular, meaningful feedback. I'm not talking about those dreaded annual reviews that everyone suffers through. I worked with a tech startup where managers had brief monthly check-ins with their teams—just fifteen minutes of focused conversation about current challenges and recent wins. Over the course of the year, their engagement scores jumped by 24%. The key wasn't the frequency alone; it was that these conversations were genuine dialogues, not one-way critiques.

There's also what I call "visibility and voice," or ensuring employees' contributions are seen and their ideas are heard. I suggest that managers highlight specific contributions from different team members during team meetings. The key part of this is that they don't just celebrate the big wins. They acknowledged the behind-the-scenes work, the problem-solving efforts, and the colleague who helped someone else meet a deadline. This practice transformed their team dynamics.

Development conversations are another critical area where many managers miss the mark. Too often, these discussions focus solely on climbing the corporate ladder. But effective managers understand that growth can take many forms. They help employees explore lateral moves, skill development, or deeper expertise in their current role. I remember a woman who was a financial analyst but didn't love the data and numbers. Instead, her passion was managing people, and she was great at it! Her supervisor helped her focus on the management side of working with people versus the data, and she later became the chief of staff responsible for all aspects of people development. Five years later, and she's still with the company, more engaged than ever.

Building Truly Inclusive Management

Manager behavior and inclusivity extend far beyond PowerPoint decks about diversity. I've seen too many organizations hide behind beautifully crafted mission statements while their day-to-day practices tell a completely different story. The reality remains clear: A manager's actions, not words, shape whether people feel truly included.

Managers who successfully build inclusive cultures ensure everyone gets airtime in meetings, not just the loudest voices. They notice when team members from different backgrounds might interpret situations differently. At a financial services company I worked with, a manager realized that his "open-door policy" wasn't working for everyone; some team members from hierarchical cultures felt uncomfortable just dropping by. His solution was to actively walk around and talk with people, and spend time at a cubicle in the middle of the department to make it easier for others to connect and chat. That's what authentic inclusion looks like in action.

A painful truth emerges repeatedly in organizations: we're setting up many managers to fail. Organizations keep promoting their best individual contributors into management roles based on technical expertise alone, then act surprised when these new managers struggle with leading diverse teams. The situation mirrors promoting someone because they're great at baking cakes and then expecting them to run a five-star restaurant. The skill sets are related but distinctly different.

This dynamic has played out at almost every company I have worked at or with. For example, a great analyst at a recruiting company was promoted to team lead without any leadership training. Six months later, half his team was looking for new jobs. Not because he wasn't brilliant at the work, but because he had never learned how to create an inclusive environment where different working styles and perspectives could thrive.

This gap in management development isn't just disappointing, it's expensive. When managers lack the skills to build inclusive teams, we see higher turnover, lower engagement, and missed opportunities for innovation. The good news is that this is fixable. Organizations that invest in real leadership development—not just a one-day workshop on unconscious bias, but ongoing support and skill building—see dramatic improvements in team performance and retention.

Success in modern organizations requires managers to move beyond surface-level inclusion efforts and implement concrete, daily practices that create genuine belonging. Through my work with dozens of organizations, I've observed specific practices that consistently drive meaningful change.

Consider the promotion process, a critical touchpoint for inclusion. Traditional approaches often favor those who self-promote or have strong informal networks. One global non-profit company

I worked with transformed its process by implementing structured nomination rounds, where managers actively identified potential candidates from all departments and backgrounds and then spent time discussing each candidate. They quickly realized that many talented individuals might have been overlooked in their previous system. By sharing those individuals in a large group, they provided opportunities for growth and development that may not have been available previously.

Project assignments often reveal hidden biases in organizations. An example of a technique used by strong inclusive managers is to track who receives high-visibility assignments and intentionally rotate these opportunities across their team. I witnessed this approach when a counseling firm started logging who led client presentations and consciously expanded their rotation, discovering that some of their most effective client communicators had previously been overlooked.

Resource allocation and development opportunities present another crucial area for inclusive practice. Forward-thinking managers ensure that training opportunities, conference attendance, and special projects are distributed equitably. They maintain transparent records of who receives these opportunities and regularly review their distribution patterns for unintended biases.

Most organizations recognize the critical importance of developing, managing, and retaining talent. They invest considerable resources in manager training programs and team-building initiatives. Yet despite this focus, many miss the mark on execution.

The promotion paradox remains one of the most persistent challenges I've observed across industries. Organizations routinely elevate their star performers into management positions based primarily on technical expertise. Picture a brilliant software engineer who writes flawless code, or an outstanding sales representative who consistently exceeds quotas. Their rewards? Management positions they may neither want nor be equipped to handle.

This approach creates a double bind: these newly minted managers often struggle without proper leadership training, while their teams suffer from inadequate support and guidance. I witnessed this scenario at a newly established museum, where a top-performing customer service representative was promoted to a leadership role. Despite her exceptional communication skills, she found herself overwhelmed by the interpersonal dynamics of managing a diverse team and didn't know how to take that skill and teach others how to be successful. The organization had essentially set her up for frustration by failing to provide the necessary management development tools.

Effective talent development requires both tactical and strategic components. Managers need practical skills like giving constructive feedback, conducting productive meetings, and managing performance issues. But they also need strategic capabilities like understanding how to build inclusive cultures, develop talent pipelines, and align team goals with organizational objectives. Unfortunately, comprehensive training in these areas proves rare. Most companies offer basic management courses that barely scratch the surface of what leaders truly need to succeed.[18]

---

18 To find out more, read The Leadership Pipeline: How to Build the Leadership Powered Company: Charan, Ram, Drotter, Stephen, Noel, James: 8601300288918: Amazon.com: Books

Creating an organized, systematic approach to talent development isn't just about checking boxes on a training schedule. It requires a fundamental shift in how organizations view management roles. Should we continue exploring specific components of effective management development programs, or would you like to examine successful models for implementing these changes?

The relationship between managers and employees forms the bedrock of organizational success. Through my research and consulting work, I've consistently found that when employees trust their managers, everything else falls into place, from performance to innovation to retention. This isn't about friendship or being everyone's favorite boss; it's about creating authentic connections built on mutual respect and genuine investment in people's growth.

I remember working with a non-profit where employee turnover had reached alarming levels. Exit interviews reinforced a common trope: people weren't leaving the company; they were leaving the managers. We implemented a comprehensive management development program focused on building trust-based leadership skills. Within 18 months, retention rates improved, not because of increased salaries or better benefits, but because managers learned to create environments where people felt seen, supported, and valued.

This brings us to the critical role of inclusive leadership training. Organizations often treat this as a "nice-to-have" addition to management development. However, my experience shows it needs to be foundational. Managers must understand both the theory and the practical application of inclusive leadership. At a Med-tech company, we developed a program where managers learned to recognize and address microaggressions, create balanced discussion environments, and ensure equitable access to opportunities. The results spoke volumes—employee engagement scores rose across all demographic groups.

Effective managers grasp that organizational culture isn't just a concept, but a lived experience shaped by daily interactions and decisions. They demonstrate this understanding through consistent actions: ensuring meeting formats accommodate different communication styles, creating multiple channels for feedback, and recognizing contributions in ways that resonate with diverse team members.

The transformation from stated values to lived reality requires concrete actions. Consider promotion processes; truly inclusive managers look beyond traditional indicators of readiness. They actively seek out potential in team members who might express ambition differently based on their cultural background or experience. They create clear, objective criteria for advancement opportunities and ensure these opportunities are communicated transparently to all team members.

These practices need to be woven into the fabric of daily operations. I have had the opportunity to work with several companies to help managers develop inclusive meeting protocols that ensured all voices were heard, not just the loudest or most senior. They implemented rotation systems for high-visibility projects and created mentoring programs that matched employees with leaders from different backgrounds. These weren't just feel-good initiatives; they drove measurable improvements in innovation, problem-solving, and team performance, as well as helped others take on leadership roles in their team.

Practice Spotlight:
Cross-Cultural Coaching

When mid-career manager Jermaine was tapped to lead a pan-European support team from his Singapore office, he struggled to get colleagues in Paris, Berlin, and Milan to speak up. Here's a practical cross-cultural coaching approach that helped him turn things around:

1. ***Assumption Audit*** *Start by listing three beliefs you hold about your international colleagues ("They won't question authority," "They prefer working alone," etc.). Calling out those blind spots upfront sets the tone for candid exploration and helps you recognize potential biases.*

2. ***Cultural Immersion Exercises*** *Book three 15-minute "perspective calls"—one with each regional rep—simply to listen. No agenda, no slides, just an invitation: "Help me understand how this looks from your end." This creates space for authentic dialogue.*

3. ***Hypothesis Testing*** *In week 3, Jermaine discovered his German colleague volunteered a process improvement, contradicting his "silent bystanders" assumption. The key is to formalize opportunities for input by creating a rotating "challenge call" slot in every meeting, explicitly asking each locale to pitch one idea.*

4. ***Feedback Loop & Reflection*** *By month 2, participation jumped by 60%, and Jermaine's team had a pipeline of region-specific suggestions. He credited the shift to simply "inviting every voice"—a small ritual with an outsized impact.*

This vignette shows that inclusive coaching isn't fluff; it's a systematic way to decode cultural nuances, surface hidden contributions, and turn geographic distance into a competitive advantage.

Methods for Inclusive Leadership in Practice

Through years of working with organizations across industries, I've identified several practical tools that help managers transform inclusive leadership from concept to reality. These aren't complex systems requiring massive organizational overhauls; they're actionable approaches that create immediate impact.

One of the most powerful ways managers can support inclusive environments is through structured check-ins with team members. These regular conversations create space for employees to share concerns, perspectives, and ideas. Effective check-ins should include questions about barriers employees are encountering, their sense of inclusion in team decisions, growth opportunities they're seeking, and how their unique perspectives could be better leveraged.

When developing inclusive management practices, organizations should focus on two key areas:

First, create assessment mechanisms that help managers understand team dynamics. This might include tracking participation patterns in meetings, examining how growth opportunities are distributed across teams, and evaluating the impact of organizational decisions on different employee groups. These data points can reveal unconscious patterns in how resources, opportunities, and attention are allocated.

Second, establish processes that actively incorporate diverse perspectives in decision-making. This means deliberately seeking input from employees with different backgrounds, experiences, and thinking styles before finalizing important decisions. As my dissertation research revealed, managers who actively seek diverse voices and perspectives help create environments where employees feel valued for their contributions and connected to their colleagues.

An important note:

When you seek input or celebrate wins, remember that not everyone is an extrovert.

Some employees love it when you stand on a table during a staff meeting and broadcast their success, or when you call on them directly in a Zoom. Others would rather dig a hole and crawl into it than speak up in a group.

As a manager, recognize that contribution styles and appreciation needs vary. Take a moment to ask each team member:

- *How do you like to be recognized?*

- *How do you want to contribute to group meetings?*

These two questions not only give you actionable answers; they also lay one more brick on the path to a trusting relationship.

The ability to build genuine relationships stands at the core of inclusive leadership. Successful managers create intentional spaces for meaningful dialogue based on mutual trust and respect. Their commitment to fairness and equality creates environments where diverse perspectives aren't just welcomed but actively sought in problem-solving processes.

Inclusive leaders also demonstrate courage by challenging biased practices and beliefs when they encounter them. This requires difficult conversations and conscious efforts to recognize and address inequities. By consistently demonstrating this commitment, managers build stronger, more cohesive teams where employees feel psychologically safe to express their authentic selves.

These behaviors combine to create environments that empower diverse talent, promote effective collaboration, and ensure all team members are treated with dignity. When managers consistently invite team members into decision-making processes, they create a truly relational approach to leadership that drives both individual and organizational success.

As we explored earlier, when employees perceive similarities between themselves and their managers, all facets of engagement are strengthened. This highlights the importance of creating connection points beyond surface-level identities, allowing team members to discover shared values, experiences, and perspectives that might not be immediately visible.

In Chapter 7, we'll look at how successful organizations are reimagining engagement for distributed teams while preserving the human connections that drive organizational success.

The Bottom Line

Hoping managers naturally know how to develop talent is like hoping your teenager will take out the trash without being asked. Manager behaviors have an outsized impact on the "I feel" and "I belong" dimensions of engagement. Most managers are promoted for technical expertise, not leadership skills—then we wonder why people leave.

The 9-Box Grid Framework: Immediate Actions You Can Take Today

Implement Regular 9-Box Reviews

Engage in manager sessions to discuss each team member:

- Where does this person sit on the performance/potential grid?
- What specific development do they need?
- What's our plan to help them grow or excel in their current role?
- Are we having honest conversations about trajectory?

Transform Development Conversations

- **Instead of vague feedback:** "You're doing fine. Keep it up."

- **Use specific, empowering language:** "You've taken real ownership of the X project, and your ability to bring the team together didn't go unnoticed. If you're interested in growing into a team lead role, let's talk through what skills you want to develop over the next six months and how I can support that."

Create the Daily Drumbeat of Engagement

Regular, Meaningful Feedback (Not Annual Reviews):

- 15-minute monthly check-ins focused on challenges and wins
- Real dialogue, not one-way critiques
- Ask: "What's working? What's not? How can I support you?"

Visibility and Voice:

- Highlight specific contributions in team meetings
- Celebrate behind-the-scenes work, not just big wins
- Ensure team members get airtime, not just the loudest voices

Development Focus:

- Growth isn't just about climbing the ladder
- Explore lateral moves, skill development, deeper expertise
- Ask: "Where do YOU want to grow?"

Build Inclusive Management Practices

Structured Check-ins Include:

- What barriers are you encountering?
- How included do you feel in team decisions?
- What growth opportunities interest you?
- How could we better leverage your unique perspective?

Equitable Opportunity Distribution:

- Track who gets high-visibility assignments
- Rotate project leadership opportunities
- Monitor training by team member
- Create transparent criteria for advancement

Meeting Inclusion Protocols:

- Send agendas in advance for preparation time
- Use rotation systems for speaking opportunities
- Ask: "How do you like to be recognized?" and "How do you prefer to contribute?"
- Create multiple channels for input (not everyone is an extrovert)

The Promotion Paradox Problem

Why Technical Experts Often Fail as Managers:

- Promoted based on individual performance, not leadership potential
- No training in coaching, feedback, or team development
- Different skill set required: building cakes ≠ running a restaurant
- Organizations assume management is a natural next step (it's not)

Solution Framework:

1. **Separate management from advancement**: Not everyone wants to lead people

2. **Require leadership training before/or right after promotion**: Management is a responsibility, not a reward

3. **Provide ongoing support**: Leadership development is continuous, not one-time

CHAPTER 6 DEVELOPING, MANAGING & RETAINING TALENT TEAR SHEET

Essential Manager Skills for Engagement

Trust-Building Behaviors:

- **Authentic Connection**: Build relationships based on mutual respect
- **Consistent Actions**: Align daily behaviors with stated values
- **Genuine Investment**: Show real interest in people's growth
- **Psychological Safety**: Create space for honest dialogue and mistakes

Inclusive Leadership Competencies:

- **Seek Diverse Perspectives**: Actively pursue different viewpoints
- **Challenge Bias**: Address inequities when encountered
- **Share Power**: Include team members in decision making
- **Cultural Competence**: Adapt communication styles to individual preferences

Development-Focused Skills:

- **Growth Conversations**: Help people see their potential and path forward
- **Resource Allocation**: Ensure equitable access to opportunities
- **Performance Coaching**: Give specific, actionable feedback
- **Career Navigation**: Help employees understand organizational dynamics

Warning Signs Your Management Development is Failing

Manager Red Flags:

- Only gives feedback during annual reviews
- Treats development conversations like checkboxes
- Promotes the loudest voices while overlooking quiet high performers
- Makes decisions without seeking diverse input
- Assumes everyone wants the same type of recognition

Organizational Red Flags:

- High turnover with exit interviews citing "manager issues"
- Promoting technical experts without leadership training
- No systematic approach to talent development
- Culture credibility gap (stated values vs. lived experience)
- Managers avoiding difficult conversations

The Trust Equation

When employees trust their managers, everything else falls into place:

- **Performance** improves because people feel safe to take risks
- **Innovation** increases because diverse perspectives are welcomed
- **Retention** rises because people feel seen and supported
- **Engagement** grows because individuals feel connected to purpose and people

Remember: Management is a Responsibility, Not a Reward

The goal isn't to create managers who are everyone's favorite boss. It's to develop leaders who:

- Create environments where people feel valued and supported
- Build authentic connections based on mutual respect
- Consistently demonstrate inclusive behaviors that drive engagement
- Balance collective team needs with individual development
- Have the courage to challenge bias and inequity when they see it

Bottom line: Talent doesn't just need to be managed—it needs to be seen, developed, and empowered to contribute authentically.

The greatest danger in times of turbulence
is not the turbulence; it is to act with yesterday's logic.
– PETER DRUCKER

CHAPTER 7

Hybrid Work Environments

Not long ago, I found myself explaining our hybrid work policy to a new hire, and she blinked in confusion. "Wait," she said, "I can pick *which* two days I come in?" Yes, I replied, and you can even put them on your calendar in neon green if that makes you happy.

Our approach wasn't born from a desire to be trendy or chase headlines; it came from hard lessons learned in the early days of post-COVID chaos. After months of trial, error, and more Zoom fatigue than I care to recall, we realized that simply dragging everyone back into the office full-time was going to be a spectacular failure. Not because people didn't want to be together, but because they wanted to be trusted. And we had to earn that trust, not mandate it.

So, here's how we structured it.

We asked employees to be in the office two days a week, but they got to choose *which* days. It wasn't a suggestion; it was an expectation, but one with built-in flexibility. The only rule? You had to note your days clearly on your calendar. That way, if your colleague was hoping to catch you in person, they didn't have to go on a scavenger hunt. It also cut down on the "Where's Jason today?" Teams messages, which, let's be honest, were getting out of hand.

We didn't assign desks either. Instead, we used a hoteling system—yes, like the one in that airport lounge you wish you had access to. Employees would "reserve" a workspace for the day. If they came in three or more days a week, they earned a permanent desk. (There may or may not have been desk envy among the two-day-a-weekers.) But overall, the system worked because it respected people's rhythms and lives outside of work.

What really made the difference wasn't the calendar invites or desk-sharing arrangements; it was the *shift in mindset*. Our managers began evaluating people not by how long they were online, but by what they produced. No more "performance by presence." If someone turned in exceptional work from a kitchen table while a toddler screamed in the background, so be it. Results became the metric that mattered.

I remember one team lead—let's call her Renee—who at first resisted this shift. She'd been in the company long enough to feel tethered to traditional models of supervision: seeing people physically at work, walking past their desks, maybe even hearing the click of keyboards as validation. But over time, she started to see something different. One of her most high-performing team members, someone she'd rarely seen in person, was delivering consistently excellent results. Meanwhile, another employee, always first to the office and last to leave, was delivering work that was . . . fine. Not bad, but not great either.

Renee had what I like to call a "sweater unraveling" moment—she pulled one thread and suddenly the whole thing came apart. She realized her assumptions about productivity were outdated. And to her credit, she adapted quickly. She started having more frequent check-ins, not to micromanage but to ask better questions: *What are you working on? Where are you stuck? How can I help?* These became the cornerstones of performance conversations.

We also reimagined our evaluation process. Rather than one big performance review at the end of the year—something that always felt like a weird combination of tax season and prom night—we moved toward regular, informal feedback loops. Managers were encouraged to acknowledge both wins and misses in real time. This did wonders for engagement. It took the pressure off the once-a-year "surprise" review and turned development into an ongoing conversation.

One thing I want to stress: this didn't happen overnight. We had to work through a lot of cultural assumptions. There was the whole "If I can't see them, are they even working?" mindset that crept up again and again. And yes, we had some people who treated work-from-home like a permanent staycation. But those were the exceptions, not the rule. Most employees stepped up because they *wanted* to succeed, and because we gave them a reason to.

What made this work? Mutual accountability.

Employees were expected to manage their schedules like grown-ups. Managers were expected to trust them like professionals. And the organization committed to evaluating people based on *impact*, not appearances.

Over time, this hybrid model started doing something surprising: it made people *more* communicative, not less. When you're not in the same room, you can't rely on hallway chatter or lunchroom gossip to stay in the loop. So, we created clear systems for communication. Weekly team huddles, shared dashboards, transparent project boards—you name it. We even implemented a few "virtual coffee roulette" pairings just to make sure people still talked to someone outside their immediate bubble.

Of course, not everything was smooth sailing. I remember one instance where an employee booked their in-office days based on when the office catered lunch (respect), while another booked theirs based on avoiding said lunch crowd. We had to iron out a few social kinks. But the larger principle held: people want autonomy, but they also want clarity. You need both for hybrid work to function.

Looking back, the shift to hybrid taught us one of the most important lessons in engagement: When people are trusted, they tend to rise to the occasion. When you focus on results instead of surveillance, you invite people to take ownership. And when you give them the space to integrate work and life in ways that are meaningful to *them*, they show up with more energy, more creativity, and more loyalty.

So, no, I don't love working from home. But I do love what a well-designed hybrid model can offer: flexibility, fairness, and most importantly, focus on what actually matters.

Engagement in a hybrid world doesn't come from ping-pong tables or mandatory virtual happy hours. It comes from the simple, radical act of saying: *I trust you to do your job well, whether I can see you or not.*

And that, my friends, is the real office evolution.

The lessons we learned from redesigning hybrid work—from choosing your own in-office days to evaluating people based on output, not hours—were just the beginning. Because the truth is, hybrid didn't appear in a vacuum. It arrived like everything else in 2020: fast, disruptive, and wearing sweatpants.

As we know, COVID transformed the way we work. It added "WFH" to our everyday language and turned our living rooms into offices overnight. Suddenly, doing laundry while listening to a work conference call, wearing a work-appropriate sweater with your pajama bottoms (aka the "work mullet"), and your fur-baby photobombing your video call became normal parts of our professional lives.

Remember when casual interactions happened organically? The catch-ups while getting coffee or the "Do you have a moment to chat" drive-bys were expected parts of the workday. These seemingly insignificant moments built relationships, solved problems, and created the social fabric that held organizations together. But what does the work-from-home lifestyle do to employee engagement? What can companies do to keep their employees connected and feeling a sense of belonging when they're scattered across different locations?

Before I go any further, I have a confession to make and it may not be popular. I'm not a fan of working from home. For me, there's something about in-office time that revitalizes me. I like the drive-bys and the quick catch-ups in the hallway. The energy of being around other people helps me think more creatively and feel more connected.

However, I recognize that my opinion isn't the norm. The data tells us that many employees have embraced remote work with open arms. The hybrid environment isn't going anywhere. So, when I'm asked about how to positively affect employee engagement in this type of environment, I give three perspectives.

Be Clear and Intentional

Remote work has stripped away the informal ways we used to stay aligned. Those casual elevator conversations where important decisions got made? Gone. The ability to read the room and adjust your approach based on people's expressions? Severely limited. In a digital environment, clarity isn't just helpful, it's essential.

Some forward-thinking organizations have found innovative ways to recreate these informal interactions virtually. Companies with remote-first cultures use dedicated Teams channels for "virtual water cooler" conversations and schedule regular non-work video hangouts. Others have implemented "virtual coffee roulette" programs that randomly pair employees for 15-minute casual conversations, mimicking those serendipitous break room encounters.

The organizations thriving in this new landscape are establishing clear communication protocols that leave nothing to chance. This means defining which communication channels to use for different interactions, because nobody needs to see your urgent "Who ate my lunch?" message on the company-wide Teams channel. Effective protocols include using email for formal announcements and decisions that need documentation, Teams for quick questions and team coordination, and video calls for complex discussions or relationship building. It means setting expectations around response times, because 3 a.m. is not an appropriate time to expect answers, no matter how many cups of coffee you've had. And it means creating meeting etiquette guidelines that acknowledge both in-office and remote participants. Yes, we can all see you eating that sandwich on camera, and no, "My video isn't working" isn't fooling anyone.

For global teams, cultural sensitivity becomes especially important. Communication styles, feedback preferences, and even meeting norms can vary dramatically across cultures. What might be considered a healthy debate in one culture could be perceived as confrontational in another. Inclusive leaders recognize these differences and create space for various communication styles while establishing shared norms that bridge cultural divides.

Asynchronous communication has emerged as a powerful tool in remote environments. Rather than requiring immediate responses, asynchronous communication allows team members to engage with information and requests when it makes sense for their schedule and cognitive capacity. This approach is particularly valuable for global teams spanning multiple time zones and for deep work that requires uninterrupted focus.

But clarity goes beyond just communication; it extends to how performance is evaluated and rewarded. The COVID-19 pandemic revealed how many of our performance evaluation systems relied on visibility rather than outcomes. In my experience as an HR practitioner, I've observed organizations suddenly realize they'd been promoting people based on presence rather than performance—those who stayed late at the office rather than those who actually delivered results.

Making promotion and evaluation criteria transparent becomes even more crucial in remote environments. This means creating clear performance benchmarks that define what good, great, and exceptional look like. It means establishing clear skill requirements for each level so there are no more guessing games. And it means outlining leadership capability requirements, because managing people is more than just approving time off.

Technology plays a crucial role in facilitating this clarity. Performance management platforms that allow for continuous feedback, goal tracking, and skill development have become essential infrastructure. These tools provide visibility into work that might otherwise go unnoticed in remote environments and create a shared understanding of expectations and progress.

As my research showed, this kind of clarity directly impacts the "I feel" and "I belong" aspects of employee engagement. When employees understand how they're being evaluated, they're more likely to feel secure and valued. My dissertation findings revealed that inclusive leadership behaviors significantly affect Shared Social Engagement (how connected employees feel to colleagues) and Positive Affective Engagement (how employees feel about their work). Specifically, my research found that inclusive leadership behaviors are positively and moderately related to shared social engagement.

The role of emotional intelligence becomes even more crucial in remote leadership. Without the benefit of body language and facial expressions that we unconsciously process in person, remote leaders need heightened awareness of emotional cues in digital communication. They must also be more intentional about expressing empathy and understanding, as the natural warmth of in-person interactions needs to be deliberately cultivated in virtual settings. Leaders with high emotional intelligence recognize when team members are struggling, even when it's not explicitly stated, and create safe spaces for authentic connection.

The most effective organizations in remote environments have implemented structured check-in systems: weekly quick connects that go deeper than just "How was your weekend?"; monthly progress reviews that catch issues before they become problems; quarterly goal alignments because plans change, and that's okay; and annual comprehensive reviews with no surprises.

However, it's essential to acknowledge the reality of "Zoom fatigue." Research from Stanford University[19] has identified four mechanisms that contribute to videoconference exhaustion: excessive close-up eye contact, constantly seeing yourself during video calls, reduced mobility, and higher cognitive load. To address this, savvy leaders are being intentional about which meetings truly require video and which could be handled through other channels. Some teams have implemented "camera-optional Fridays" or audio-only walking meetings to reduce screen time while maintaining connection.

Remote work affects different personality types in vastly different ways. Introverts may thrive in the reduced social stimulation of remote work, finding they can focus better and contribute more thoughtfully in virtual settings where they can process their thoughts before speaking. Extroverts, meanwhile, may struggle with reduced social interaction and spontaneous connection. Inclusive leaders recognize these differences and create environments that work for both types, providing quiet focus time and independent work for introverts while creating optional social connection points for extroverts who crave interaction.

19 Fauville, G., Luo, M., Queiroz, A. C. M., Bailenson, J. N., & Hancock, J. (2021). Zoom Exhaustion & Fatigue Scale. Computers in Human Behavior Reports, 4, 100119. https://doi.org/10.1016/j.chbr.2021.100119.

These aren't just administrative tasks, they're engagement opportunities. Each touchpoint is a chance to reinforce connection, provide recognition, and ensure alignment. As my dissertation research revealed, "shared social engagement," or how connected employees feel to their colleagues through shared values and goals, is significantly impacted by leadership behaviors. Regular, structured check-ins help maintain this connection when spontaneous interactions aren't possible.

Many organizations are finding that hybrid work models offer the best of both worlds. By designating specific days for in-office collaboration while allowing flexibility for remote work, companies can leverage the focus and flexibility benefits of remote work while maintaining the relationship-building and spontaneous innovation advantages of in-person interaction. The key to successful hybrid models lies in being intentional about when and why people come together, rather than requiring office presence without purpose.

Work-life balance takes on new meaning in remote environments, where the boundaries between personal and professional life can easily blur. Without the physical separation of commuting to an office, many remote workers struggle to "turn off" at the end of the day. Inclusive leaders model healthy boundaries by respecting after-hours time, being clear about expectations for availability, and encouraging employees to create rituals to mark the transition between work and personal time. Some teams have implemented "virtual commutes"—short meditations or reflections at the beginning and end of the day to create psychological separation between work and home life.

Feedback mechanisms also become crucial in remote

environments. Create systems where peers can give feedback, people can "humble brag" about themselves, and managers can also hear how they're doing (because managers need feedback too). These mechanisms create the psychological safety that Kahn (1990) identified as essential for engagement.

Ensure Inclusive Decision-Making

Clarity in remote environments must extend to how decisions are made. The old world of hallway conversations and impromptu meetings created decision-making inequities that remote work can either exacerbate or help solve. Goodbye, water cooler politics. Remote work allows us to create more transparent, inclusive decision-making processes that engage employees regardless of location.

My research consistently shows that when employees understand how and why decisions are made, they're more likely to feel engaged, even if they don't agree with every outcome. This directly connects to the Shared Social Engagement dimension of employee engagement identified in my dissertation. When decisions happen in visible, accessible ways, employees feel connected to the organization's goals and mission.

Creating a central digital space where all significant decisions are documented is essential. Tools like Confluence, Notion, or dedicated decision management platforms like Crayon can create this shared repository (and no, they are not paying me to plug them). You could also establish a structured decision-making process and document key decisions in Google Docs or Microsoft Word, stored in a central location like SharePoint.

Hybrid environments present unique challenges for inclusive

decision-making. When some team members are physically together while others are remote, the in-office group naturally forms an information and decision-making advantage. I've observed organizations combating this by implementing a "digital-first" approach where all decisions are documented in shared digital spaces, even when some participants are physically together. Some teams even maintain a video connection with remote colleagues during in-office discussions to prevent the formation of information silos.

Decision protocols become even more important in hybrid environments. The RACI framework (Responsible, Accountable, Consulted, Informed) provides a structured approach to clarifying who needs to be involved in what capacity for different types of decisions. These protocols create clarity about whose input is needed and who makes the final call, preventing both decision paralysis and executive overreach.

Digital collaboration tools can enable real-time input from distributed teams while asynchronous feedback channels ensure that people in different time zones can contribute meaningfully. This means scheduling meetings at times that work across locations and providing multiple ways for people to share their perspectives before decisions are finalized.

Of course, complete transparency isn't always possible or desirable. Certain decisions involve confidential information about personnel, legal matters, or strategic initiatives that can't be broadly shared. Additionally, too much information can lead to cognitive overload, where employees struggle to separate signals from noise. The most effective organizations establish clear guidelines about what types of decisions will be shared, in what format, and with what level of detail.

Regular updates to all stakeholders maintain alignment and engagement. As my research demonstrated, employees need to understand not only what was decided but also the reasoning behind it. "We chose this because we threw darts at a board" is technically transparent, but maybe not ideal. Sharing the decision-making process, including the alternatives considered and the criteria used, builds trust and helps employees understand the "why" behind organizational choices.

Training leaders and employees to participate effectively in inclusive decision-making is critical. This includes developing skills in asynchronous communication, digital collaboration, and inclusive facilitation. Leaders need to learn how to draw out perspectives from remote participants who might otherwise remain silent, while employees need guidance on how to contribute effectively in digital forums. My research indicates that when organizations invest in these capabilities, they see corresponding increases in employee engagement scores.

Decision fatigue is a real concern when trying to implement inclusive processes. Not every decision warrants broad input, and attempting to include everyone in everything quickly leads to burnout and inefficiency. Organizations need a tiered approach that distinguishes between decisions that require broad input (strategic direction, major process changes) versus those that can be handled through delegation or individual authority (day-to-day operational decisions). The RACI framework mentioned earlier provides a structured way to make these distinctions.

Many leaders have found success holding regular "Ask Me

Anything" sessions where employees can submit questions anonymously or directly. These sessions create forums for honest dialogue that can address concerns before they become disengagement drivers. My dissertation findings about Positive Affective Engagement highlight how emotional connection to work is strengthened when employees feel heard and respected.

For these sessions to be effective, clear ground rules need to be established while keeping them authentic. Leaders should be transparent about what's off-limits (legal issues, personnel matters, that time you danced at the holiday party) and what happens with unanswered questions. The most successful leaders research current company issues and hot topics, preparing thoughtful responses to the questions that are likely on employees' minds.

Those tough questions are coming: "Why did we *really* reorganize the department?" "Are we planning layoffs?" "Why did an executive leave suddenly?" "Do you believe in our company values?" "When are we getting real raises?" "What keeps you up at night about our company?" The way leaders address these questions—with honesty, empathy, and appropriate transparency—directly affects how engaged employees feel.

Having a "parking lot" strategy for questions needing follow-up is essential for making these sessions productive while ensuring no question gets lost. This approach acknowledges questions that can't be immediately addressed while creating accountability for following up. Leaders should clearly explain which questions they're "parking," who will be responsible for the follow-up, and when participants can expect an answer. When you promise to follow up, do it. Nothing erodes trust faster than forgotten commitments.

Be honest when you don't know something. In remote environments where authenticity is currency, attempting to bluff through uncertainty damages credibility. My research on inclusive leadership shows that vulnerability—acknowledging limits and seeking input—creates psychological safety that encourages others to contribute openly. When you say, "I don't know, but I'll find out," make sure you actually do find out and share what you learn.

Know when to take a question offline. Some topics are too complex, sensitive, or specific for group settings. Rather than dismissing these questions, acknowledge their importance and set up appropriate channels to address them. This demonstrates respect both for the questioner and the broader audience while ensuring important concerns don't get sidelined.

Offer multiple channels for questions: live during sessions, anonymously through digital tools, or pre-submitted for those who need time to formulate their thoughts. This creates accessibility for different communication styles and preferences, supporting the inclusive leadership principle of "actively seeking out diverse voices and perspectives" that my research identified as crucial for engagement.

Record sessions for those who can't attend live and provide written summaries of key points for those who prefer reading to watching. This ensures information reaches everyone regardless of schedule constraints, time zones, or learning preferences. This addresses the "I belong" aspect of engagement that my research highlighted as critical for remote workers who might otherwise feel disconnected.

Provide regular updates on action items from previous sessions. This closes the communication loop and demonstrates that these forums aren't just performative, but lead to meaningful action. My dissertation findings indicate that when employees see their input making a difference, their engagement increases significantly, creating a virtuous cycle of participation and action.

Measuring the effectiveness of inclusive decision-making processes requires concrete metrics. Organizations can track metrics like time-to-decision (to ensure inclusive processes don't create paralysis), decision quality (measured through post-implementation reviews), employee feedback on decision processes (through pulse surveys), and engagement scores correlated with perceptions of decision inclusivity. These metrics provide tangible ways to assess whether inclusive approaches are working as intended.

Inclusive decision-making in remote environments can significantly impact innovation and creativity. My research on inclusive leadership shows that when diverse perspectives are actively sought and incorporated, teams develop more creative solutions and identify potential issues earlier. In remote settings, this means using digital brainstorming tools that allow for both synchronous and asynchronous ideation, ensuring that the best ideas emerge regardless of where people are located or when they're working.

This connects directly to the findings in my dissertation regarding manager behaviors and engagement. When managers exhibit inclusive behaviors such as actively seeking diverse perspectives, challenging systematic processes for fairness, and facilitating honest dialogue, employees report higher levels of engagement. In remote environments, these inclusive behaviors must be even more intentional and visible.

The transparency created by documenting decisions, establishing clear protocols, and holding open forums addresses one of the primary concerns I heard in my research about remote work: the fear of being "out of the loop." By making decision-making processes visible and accessible to all, organizations can ensure that physical distance doesn't create engagement distance.

This approach to inclusive decision-making builds upon the clarity we discussed earlier. When employees understand not only what's expected of them but also how organizational decisions are made, they develop a deeper sense of belonging and connection. As my research demonstrated, this belonging is a critical component of engagement, particularly for employees from underrepresented groups who may already feel marginalized in organizational contexts.

Lead with Connection

If there's one thing I've learned in my 25 years in HR, it's that connection isn't just nice to have, it's the oxygen of engagement. And just like oxygen, you don't notice it until it's gone. Post-pandemic, we've all come to realize that those casual hallway conversations we took for granted were actually the invisible threads holding our workplace relationships together.

Remote work has forced managers to master a whole new skill set: virtual communication, building trust without physical proximity, and managing performance based on outcomes rather than observation. Let me tell you, this is no small feat. It's like learning to parallel park all over again, but this time blindfolded and with someone shouting directions through a bad Zoom connection.

Research in Action: Cross-National Knowledge Sharing

Imagine a product-development squad split between Mumbai, Munich, and Montreal—kind of like scheduling dinner for your extended family when half the guests are three time zones away, except with fewer scalloped potatoes and more Gantt charts. In their 2018 study, Bodla, Tang, Jiang, and Tian found that simply assembling diverse team members isn't enough. What really moves the needle is cultivating an explicit knowledge-sharing climate alongside an inclusive team culture.

In practice, that looked like two daily rituals even the shyest networker couldn't dodge: A quick 10-minute "Knowledge Pulse" huddle, where every site (yes, even that one guy who thinks mute is his best friend) shares one insight or pain point.

A rotating "Cultural Spotlight" (think less tourist brochure, more "Tell us why your vendor's week-long holiday matters so we don't look like schmendriks when we schedule a launch") where one office briefs the others on local quirks.

The outcome? Teams in the Bodla et al. study boasted 25 % higher innovation scores and prototyped new ideas twice as fast compared to groups without these rituals.

It's proof that inclusion isn't just schmaltz, but the spark that ignites collaboration, and a little intentional ritual can turn those time-zone headaches into golden opportunities.

Organizations are placing greater emphasis on emotional intelligence and empathy in leadership development. The ability to understand and respond to employee needs, create psychological safety, and foster inclusion has become crucial for effective leadership. Managers who excel at creating connection see significantly higher engagement scores across all dimensions.

So, how do we create these connections in the brave new world of hybrid work? First, we need to create opportunities for informal communication. And no, sending memes in the team chat doesn't count as a strategy, though I've seen worse attempts, believe me. We need intentional structures that recreate those serendipitous encounters that used to happen naturally.

Try scheduling 15-minute "coffee roulette" sessions that pair random team members for quick virtual coffees. I know a financial services company that implemented this and saw cross-departmental collaboration increase by 34%. Or start themed Teams channels beyond work topics (#pet-pictures is always a winner, though I'm still traumatized by the iguana someone on my team apparently keeps as a "cuddle buddy.") Each of these touchpoints creates small bridges between the isolated islands we can become when working remotely.

Host virtual lunch hours where the only rule is no work talk. Yes, we will judge your choice of sandwich, and yes, that's part of the fun. These seemingly trivial interactions build the foundation for deeper connection. Shared Social Engagement—how connected employees feel to their colleagues through shared values and goals—significantly impacts overall engagement.

Another approach is implementing "Walk and Talk" meetings where everyone takes their 1:1s while walking outside. Bonus: no one can share their screen with 47 PowerPoint slides. Movement activates different parts of the brain, leading to more creative thinking and authentic conversation. As my grandmother would say, "You want a good talk? Take a good walk."

Being vulnerable might be the most powerful connection tool in your kit. Share personal challenges and lessons learned, like that time you forgot to unmute for an entire presentation, or admit when you don't have all the answers (shocking, I know). My research demonstrates that when leaders model vulnerability, psychological safety increases dramatically, and employees feel more comfortable bringing their whole selves to work.

Establish "No Judgment Zones" for brainstorming. We listen and we don't judge, which, let me tell you, is the opposite of how I was raised in New York, where judging was practically the official state sport. But in these safe spaces, innovation flourishes because people aren't afraid to share half-baked ideas that might evolve into brilliant solutions.

Creating team traditions that work in hybrid settings can be powerful connection points. Monthly Pet Parade, anyone? Yes, it sounds ridiculous, and that's partly why it works. These lightweight, fun rituals create shared experiences that bind teams together regardless of location. In my team, we do "Weekly Wins and Whoops" where everyone shares a success and a mistake. Because perfection is overrated and learning from mistakes is underrated.

Keep Learning

The second pillar of remote engagement is continuous learning. As technological change accelerates, skills development becomes increasingly crucial. Organizations need to invest more in ongoing learning, potentially shifting toward skills-based rather than role-based organizational structures.

Create microlearning moments like "Tech Tuesday" tips shared via team channels. Finally, understand what that mysterious button does in your CRM system! Or try sharing "Fail Forward" stories where team members discuss lessons learned. Turns out, sending that email to the entire company instead of just Janet was quite the learning opportunity, wasn't it, Steve?

Devise skill-based learning tracks where people can access cross-functional training. Sometimes the best Excel guru is hiding in the marketing department, like my colleague Pat, who somehow turned a spreadsheet into what I can only describe as a work of technological wizardry. Organize "skill swap" sessions where team members teach each other their superpowers . . . because everyone has at least one.

Encourage personal development time where employees can allocate dedicated "learning hours" to new skills. Even if it's learning to code just to automate your daily reports, which, between us, is exactly what I did with those monthly engagement metrics that used to take me hours. My boss thought I was a magician, but really, I just got tired of doing the same mind-numbing task every month. Work smarter, not harder, as my father always said (usually while finding the shortest line at Zabar's).

Develop peer learning programs or "Knowledge Networks" where experts can be easily found. Turns out John in accounting is an Excel shortcuts wizard, and now he's teaching half the company how to use VLOOKUP without breaking into a cold sweat. These networks democratize learning, making expertise accessible regardless of hierarchy or location.

Create problem-solving competitions or develop team case studies based on real scenarios. Like that time the entire system went down right before the quarterly all-hands meeting. These practical learning experiences build both skills and camaraderie as teams work through challenges together.

Match people who know stuff with people who want to know stuff through mentor-mentee programs based on skills and goals (not just who has the most impressive Zoom background). Try "Reverse Mentoring" where junior staff teach senior leaders. Yes, they need to learn what TikTok is, if only to understand why the interns keep doing that dance move during coffee breaks.

Make learning stick by creating opportunities to immediately apply new skills. Implement "Skill of the Month" challenges where everyone practices the same new capability, creating a shared learning experience that builds connection while developing capabilities.

Remember to recognize and reward those who continue to learn. Celebrate learning milestones beyond just adding another certification to email signatures. Implement skill-based advancement opportunities or reward knowledge sharing and teaching others.

One quick note: not everyone sees recognition the same way. Before you stand up in the middle of a staff meeting to congratulate Damon on his new certification or Pat on their latest achievement, take the time to learn how your team wants to be recognized. I had a conversation with my team where I asked them that question: one team member wanted their desk decorated in recognition of achievement, and the other preferred that I just say, "Great job, congratulations" to them directly without any hoopla. It is their recognition, so deliver it in the way that makes them feel the best. You know what my Grandmother would say: "It's not about the recognition you want to give; it's about the recognition they want to receive." Grandma wasn't in HR, but she would have made a killer engagement consultant.

The beauty of learning in remote environments is that it serves double duty, building both capabilities and connections. When we learn together, even virtually, we create shared experiences that strengthen bonds while developing the skills needed for future success. My research consistently shows that organizations that prioritize both connection and learning see significantly higher engagement scores across all dimensions, even in fully remote settings.

The hybrid work revolution has fundamentally transformed how we think about engagement, connection, and productivity. As organizations navigate this new terrain, success hinges not on recreating office dynamics in digital spaces but on reimagining engagement through the lens of flexibility, intentionality, and inclusion.

The most successful organizations recognize that hybrid work isn't a temporary adjustment but a strategic advantage that can drive innovation, expand talent pools, and enhance employee satisfaction when implemented thoughtfully. By prioritizing clear communication, fostering genuine connection across physical boundaries, and continuously evolving policies based on employee feedback, organizations can create environments where team members thrive regardless of their physical location.

As we move forward, the organizations that will excel aren't those clinging to traditional models or hastily embracing remote-first approaches, but those willing to experiment, learn, and adapt, creating workplaces that harness the best of both worlds while mitigating their challenges. The future of work is neither fully remote nor strictly in-person. It's a dynamic, evolving blend that puts people and their diverse needs at the center.

The Bottom Line

Hybrid work isn't about recreating office dynamics in digital spaces—it's about reimagining engagement through flexibility, intentionality, and inclusion. Success comes from trusting people to do their jobs well, whether you can see them or not. Results matter more than presence.

The Three Pillars of Hybrid Engagement

1. Be Clear and Intentional

Replace informal alignment with structured communication:

- Define communication protocols for different channels and purposes
- Set clear expectations for response times and availability
- Create transparent performance benchmarks based on outcomes, not hours
- Establish meeting etiquette that includes both remote and in-office participants

2. Ensure Inclusive Decision-Making

Make decision processes visible and accessible to all:

- Document decisions in central digital spaces everyone can access
- Use structured frameworks (like RACI) to clarify roles in decisions
- Hold regular "Ask Me Anything" sessions for transparent dialogue
- Provide multiple channels for input (live, asynchronous, anonymous)

3. Lead with Connection

Create intentional opportunities for relationship building:

- Create intentional pairings for cross-team connections
- Host virtual lunch hours with no work talk allowed
- Implement "Walk and Talk" meetings for 1:1s
- Share vulnerabilities and model psychological safety

Immediate Actions You Can Take Today

Audit Your Hybrid Setup

Ask these critical questions:

- Do remote employees have equal access to information and opportunities?
- Are we evaluating people on results or perceived productivity?
- Do our meeting formats work for both in-person and remote participants?
- Are informal networks and decision-making creating proximity bias?

Establish Communication Protocols

Channel Clarity:

- **Email**: Formal announcements, documented decisions
- **Slack/Teams**: Quick questions, team coordination, daily updates
- **Video calls**: Complex discussions, relationship building, brainstorming
- **Asynchronous tools**: Deep work feedback, global team input

Meeting Standards:

- Send agendas 24 hours in advance
- Start with connection (not just "Can everyone hear me?")
- Use "digital-first" approach even when some are co-located
- Record sessions for those in different time zones

Design Your Hybrid Model

Flexible Office Presence:

- Let employees choose their in-office days (with calendar transparency)
- Use hoteling systems for desk assignments
- Reserve permanent desks for employees who come in 3+ days
- Create clear expectations: guidance, not surveillance

Performance Management:

- Shift from "performance by presence" to results-based evaluation
- Implement regular check-ins (weekly, monthly, quarterly)
- Focus on impact and outcomes, not hours logged
- Create clear skill and leadership requirements for advancement

Create Connection Rituals

Informal Interaction Replacements:

- **Themed Teams channels**: #pet-pictures, #weekend-adventures, #book-club

- **Virtual lunch hours**: No work talk, just relationship building
- **"Knowledge Networks"**: Connect people who know stuff with people who want to learn

Team Traditions:

- **Weekly Wins and Whoops**: Share successes and learning moments
- **Monthly Pet Parade**: Light, fun shared experiences
- **Skill of the Month**: Everyone learns something new together
- **"Fail Forward" stories**: Normalize learning from mistakes

Implement Inclusive Decision Protocols

Documentation Standards:

- Create central repository for all significant decisions
- Include reasoning behind choices, not just outcomes
- Share alternatives considered and criteria used
- Provide tiered access based on confidentiality needs

Input Mechanisms:

- **RACI framework**: Clarify who's Responsible, Accountable, Consulted, Informed
- **Asynchronous feedback**: Allow time-zone flexibility for input
- **Anonymous channels**: Safe spaces for honest feedback
- **Regular AMAs**: Address concerns before they become disengagement

Recognition Approaches:
- Ask each person: "How do you like to be recognized?"
- Celebrate learning milestones, not just certifications
- Reward knowledge sharing and teaching others
- Create skill-based advancement opportunities

Measuring Hybrid Success

Engagement Indicators:
- **Shared Social Engagement**: How connected do people feel to colleagues?
- **Positive Affective Engagement**: Do people feel good about their work?
- **Inclusion metrics**: Equal access to opportunities and information?
- **Performance outcomes**: Are results improving regardless of location?

Warning Signs Your Hybrid Model is Failing

Proximity Bias Red Flags:
- In-office employees get more opportunities or information
- Decisions happen in hallway conversations
- Remote employees are "forgotten" in meeting invitations
- Performance evaluations favor visible over valuable work

Connection Breakdown Indicators:
- Decreased cross-team collaboration
- Employees feel isolated or "out of the loop"
- Informal networks only include co-located workers
- Innovation and creativity declining

Communication Failures:
- Important information shared inconsistently
- Meeting formats exclude remote participants
- Feedback loops broken or one-directional
- Time zone differences creating information gaps

The Cultural Sensitivity Factor

For Global Teams:
- Recognize communication style differences across cultures
- Accommodate various feedback preferences and meeting norms
- Create space for different approaches to collaboration
- Bridge cultural divides with shared digital-first practices

Asynchronous Advantages:
- Allows thoughtful contribution regardless of time zones
- Supports deep work without constant interruption
- Accommodates different cognitive styles and energy patterns
- Creates inclusive opportunities for introverted team members

Technology as Engagement Infrastructure

Essential Digital Tools:

- **Performance management platforms**: Continuous feedback and goal tracking

- **Collaboration spaces**: Shared documents, project boards, decision logs

- **Communication hubs**: Multiple channels for different interaction types

- **Learning platforms**: Skill development and knowledge sharing

"Zoom Fatigue" Solutions:

- Make video optional when appropriate

- Implement "camera-optional Fridays"

- Use audio-only walking meetings

Remember: Trust is the Foundation

Mutual Accountability Framework:

- **Employees**: Manage schedules professionally, communicate proactively

- **Managers**: Focus on outcomes, provide clear expectations and support

- **Organization**: Evaluate based on impact, invest in infrastructure and training

The Engagement Truth: When people are trusted to do their jobs well, given clear expectations, and provided meaningful connections to colleagues and purpose, they thrive regardless of where they sit.

CHAPTER 7 HYBRID WORK ENVIRONMENTS TEAR SHEET

Key Success Factors

1. **Design for inclusion**: Prevent proximity bias while leveraging diverse perspectives

2. **Lead with intentionality**: Replace casual interactions with purposeful connection

3. **Embrace asynchronous work**: Shift to outcome-based productivity measures

4. **Foster digital fluency**: Invest in technology and capabilities for seamless collaboration

5. **Continuously adapt**: Gather feedback and refine approaches based on evolving needs

Bottom line: The future of work isn't fully remote or strictly in-person—it's a dynamic blend that puts people and their diverse needs at the center.

"The future of AI needs to be human-centered."
– DR. FEI-FEI LI

CHAPTER 8

AI's Role in Engagement: The Future Unveiled

A few years ago, I was working with a large public-sector organization—let's call them "Grew Systems"—that had a very clear problem: their employee engagement scores were falling year after year. And not by a little. The numbers were heading south with a velocity that made it hard to blame just the weather, the workload, or the occasional cranky department head.

So, I asked to see their data. What I got was a beautifully formatted PowerPoint full of bar graphs and Net Promoter Scores—color-coded, even! But there was one glaring issue: no context.

"What's missing?" I asked.

"Well," said the head of HR, "we don't do open-text responses. Too messy. Legal's not a fan."

Right.

Their entire engagement strategy was based on multiple-choice surveys. The kind where you get five options ranging from "Strongly Agree" to "Strongly Disagree" and then are somehow supposed to divine employee sentiment from that alone. The result? A flood of generic feedback: vague grumblings about "leadership," "communication," or "culture" without any specifics about *what* was broken, *where*, or *why*.

Think of it like trying to understand your partner's feelings based only on whether they checked "I'm fine" or "Not fine" on a sticky note. It doesn't get you very far.

So, I made a recommendation that seemed simple enough: add open-text boxes. Let people explain what's really going on. Then, feed that data into an AI tool, like ChatGPT or Claude, and see what themes emerge.[20] We weren't asking AI to make decisions, just to help *decode* what thousands of employees were saying.

The idea was to spark conversations, not replace them. The tool could identify repeated patterns: leadership trust issues in one division, communication breakdowns in another, and burnout among middle managers. Then the humans could do what humans do best: ask more questions, prioritize, and take meaningful action.

But here's the twist: they didn't do it.

Legal shut it down over data retention policies, and leadership got cold feet. The concern? "What if we find out something we don't want to know?"

Which, of course, was exactly the point.

Instead, they continued with checkbox surveys and watched

---

20 OpenAI. "Introducing ChatGPT." OpenAI, November 2022. https://openai.com/blog/chatgpt.

their engagement scores tank another year in a row.

Now contrast that with a different organization I worked with—let's call them Pacific Technologies. They embraced AI early but wisely. Instead of just measuring satisfaction once a year, they installed a lightweight AI-powered feedback system that could gather real-time, natural language responses from employees. People could vent, praise, critique, or suggest in their own words. And the system would sort, summarize, and surface patterns leaders could act on.

Here's what was surprising but not shocking: the AI flagged something leadership had completely missed. Engagement was tanking on one team, not because of compensation, workload, or even a bad manager, but because recurring all-hands meetings were being scheduled over school pickup hours. Parents were having to choose between staying visible and showing up for their kids. A small thing with big consequences.[21] And the fix? Also small. They moved the meetings by 30 minutes.

Boom. Problem solved. Not by magic, but by *context*.

This is what excites me about AI in the engagement space: not flashy dashboards or predictive buzzwords, but the ability to surface human nuance at scale.

Of course, none of this means AI replaces leaders or HR professionals. On the contrary. What I've found in every successful implementation is that the *best* outcomes happen when AI insights are used to prompt human conversations, not shortcut them.

It's the same philosophy I used in another engagement with a financial services firm. We used AI to analyze multi-year survey

---

21 Reichheld, Fred. The Ultimate Question 2.0: How Net Promoter Companies Thrive in a Customer-Driven World. Boston: Harvard Business Review Press, 2011.

data and categorize feedback by emotional tone. What we found was illuminating: "disappointment" had replaced "frustration" as the dominant emotional keyword. That shift may seem subtle, but it's huge. Frustration implies hope that things might change. Disappointment means people have given up. And when your workforce stops complaining? You're in trouble.

We used that insight to prioritize manager training and peer recognition programs, which helped reset the emotional tone across the org. Within a year, engagement scores rebounded for the first time in four years.

Now, is AI perfect? Of course not. It can miss sarcasm (which, as you may have noticed, is my native language). It can get tripped up by context, and it's only as good as the data it's trained on. But when paired with human judgment and a bit of courage, it becomes a powerful partner in engagement strategy.[22]

Let me be clear about one thing, though: this isn't plug-and-play. AI works best when you're clear about the *problem* you're trying to solve. That's why I encourage leaders to ask the following before implementing any engagement tech:

- What are we hoping to learn that we don't already know?
- How will this information influence decisions or policies?
- Who will own the follow-up?
- What will success look like?

---

22 Bloom, Nicholas, et al. "The Benefits of Working From Home." Stanford Institute for Economic Policy Research, March 2021. https://siepr.stanford.edu/publications/working-papers/benefits-working-home.

Because AI that generates insights no one acts on? That's just digital furniture. Looks impressive. Doesn't do much.

And yes, there are ethical considerations. Privacy, transparency, and fairness all matter. Employees need to know their words won't be weaponized. That their feedback, especially in open text, will be used for good, not for retaliation. That's why any AI tool should be paired with a clear governance plan, communication strategy, and training for the people interpreting the results.[23]

What I've learned across all these engagements is simple: AI doesn't need to replace the human touch. It needs to *enhance* it. To help us see patterns faster, hear voices more clearly, and respond with greater precision and empathy.

Because, real engagement? That comes from people. AI just helps us listen better.

Those real-world examples only scratch the surface of what AI can do when it's designed and deployed thoughtfully. But they also raise a deeper question: What exactly is AI changing when it comes to how people engage with work? To answer that, we have to zoom out from the tools and look at the terrain. Because what we're dealing with isn't just new technology; it's a new relationship between humans and the systems that shape their daily experience.

---

23 Schwartz, Jeff, et al. "2020 Global Human Capital Trends." Deloitte Insights, 2020. https://www2.deloitte.com/insights.

Checkbox Surveys vs. Open-Text + AI Analysis

Method	Checkbox Surveys	Open-Text + AI Analysis
Depth of Insight	Shallow, pre-defined responses	Rich, nuanced employee voice
Bias Risk	High – limits responses to what's anticipated	Lower – employees speak in their own language
Ease of Analysis	Easy but limited	Complex but deeper – requires processing
Emotion Detection	None or inferred from scale	Can identify emotional tone via sentiment analysis
Surprise Factors	Rare – leaders only get what they ask	High – themes can emerge that leaders didn't expect
Scalability	Easy for large populations	Scalable with AI support
Actionability	Often vague ("Improve communication")	Clearer insight into what and where to act

The intersection of artificial intelligence and employee engagement represents one of the most fascinating and complex challenges facing organizations today. As we explore this territory, we need to understand both the transformative potential and the human implications of AI in the workplace. Through my research and consulting work, I've identified three distinct pathways where AI significantly impacts employee engagement, particularly in how people think, feel, and connect with their work.

The first pathway centers on how AI transforms individual learning and development. When employees have access to AI-powered learning tools that adapt to their unique needs and pace, we see a powerful convergence of technology and human potential. This isn't just about accessing information, but about creating personalized learning journeys that respond and evolve with each employee's progress.

Consider the relationship between AI-enhanced learning and author Carol Dweck's concept of growth mindset (*Mindset: The New Psychology of Success, 2007*). When employees believe in their ability to develop new skills (growth mindset) and have access to AI tools that provide customized learning pathways, we create what I call a "development accelerator." I witnessed this at Global Tech, where implementing AI-driven learning platforms didn't just improve skill acquisition but fundamentally shifted how employees viewed their own potential for growth.

The second pathway involves AI's transformation of core HR processes throughout the employee lifecycle. From recruitment through onboarding and beyond, AI tools can enhance how employees connect with and navigate their organizational experience.

However—and this is crucial—technology must serve as an enabler of human connection, not a replacement for it.

In my work with forward-thinking organizations, I've observed how thoughtfully implemented AI can strengthen the "I belong" aspect of engagement. For instance, AI-enhanced onboarding systems can help new hires better understand and connect with organizational culture, while smart scheduling tools can facilitate more meaningful face-to-face interactions.

Balancing Fear and Value

This brings us to perhaps the most critical aspect of AI implementation: managing the delicate balance between technological advancement and human concerns. HR professionals face a crucial responsibility in this area. Based on my research and field experience, successful organizations address this challenge through four key approaches:

1. **Clear Communication of Purpose:** Organizations must articulate exactly how and why they're implementing AI tools. Rather than making vague statements about innovation, successful leaders connect AI initiatives to specific, tangible improvements in employee experience.

2. **Strategic Alignment:** Every AI implementation needs clear links to organizational goals. This isn't about technology for technology's sake. It's about purposeful adoption that advances both individual and organizational objectives.

3. Governance and Oversight: Clear frameworks for AI usage help ensure these tools enhance rather than diminish the human element of work. This includes establishing guidelines for ethical AI use and regular assessments of impact on employee experience.

4. Individual Development Integration: The most successful organizations integrate AI tools into personal development plans thoughtfully. Like the example of using Grammarly for writing improvement, the key is connecting technological assistance to concrete skill development goals.

Implementing AI for Meaningful Engagement

The successful integration of AI into organizational engagement strategies requires more than just selecting the right tools; it demands a thoughtful approach to implementation that preserves and enhances human connection. Through my research with organizations across sectors, I've identified several key patterns that differentiate successful AI adoption from initiatives that fall short.

Consider how Starbucks uses their Deep Brew AI system to predict customer preferences and optimize inventory.[24] Baristas receive AI-powered insights about likely orders, allowing them to focus on customer interaction rather than guessing preferences. Employee engagement scores in pilot stores increased as staff felt more equipped to provide personalized service.

---

24 Starbucks Corporation. (2019). "Starbucks Announces Q4 and Full Year Fiscal 2019 Results." Starbucks Investor Relations.

The Learning Partnership

What makes AI particularly powerful in the engagement sphere is its ability to create what I call "learning partnerships" with employees. Unlike traditional training programs that follow a one-size-fits-all approach, AI-enhanced learning systems adapt to individual learning patterns and preferences. At Global Financial, they implemented an AI-driven professional development platform that tracks not just completion rates but learning styles and application patterns. The system suggests personalized learning paths based on an employee's role, goals, and demonstrated strengths.

But here's the crucial distinction: Successful organizations position AI as a complement to, not a replacement for, human development relationships. The technology serves as an enabler, providing insights that managers and mentors can use to have more meaningful development conversations with their team members.

One of the most challenging aspects of AI implementation involves measuring its impact on engagement. Through my consulting work, I've developed a framework that helps organizations assess both quantitative and qualitative outcomes. This includes:

- Tracking changes in employee sentiment before and after AI implementation

- Measuring productivity gains while monitoring stress levels

- Assessing the quality of human interactions in AI-enhanced processes

- Evaluating the depth and effectiveness of personalized learning experience. The key is maintaining what

I call "human-centered metrics"—measurements that go beyond efficiency to capture the actual impact on employee experience and engagement.

Understanding AI Fundamentals in HR

Before diving deeper into AI's impact on engagement, we need to establish a clear foundation. AI represents the broader concept of machines performing tasks that typically require human intelligence. Machine Learning, a subset of AI, focuses on systems that learn from data patterns to make predictions or decisions. This distinction matters because different HR applications require different approaches.

The power of AI in understanding employee engagement extends beyond traditional survey methods. Through advanced analytics and natural language processing, organizations can now gather and interpret employee sentiment in real-time. At Pacific Technologies, their AI-powered feedback system identified engagement patterns that traditional surveys had missed entirely. For instance, they discovered that team meeting schedules significantly impacted engagement levels—something that wouldn't have been apparent through annual surveys alone.

Ethical Considerations in AI Implementation

As we integrate AI into engagement strategies, ethical considerations must remain paramount. Privacy protection, data security, and decision-making transparency form the cornerstone of responsible AI implementation. Organizations must establish clear governance frameworks addressing crucial questions about data access, bias prevention, and employee protection. The most successful organizations create comprehensive policies that balance innovation with ethical responsibility.

The integration of AI into HR practices isn't just changing how we work, it's transforming the HR profession itself. Today's HR professionals need to develop new competencies to effectively leverage AI tools while maintaining the human element of their role. This includes developing a deep understanding of AI capabilities and limitations, building skills in interpreting AI-generated insights, and mastering the delicate balance between technological efficiency and human connection.

At Global Financial, HR leaders undergo quarterly training to stay current with AI developments, ensuring they can make informed decisions about technology implementation while preserving the human touch in their interactions. This ongoing education enables them to serve as bridges between technological capability and human needs, ensuring that AI enhances rather than replaces meaningful human connections.

The future of AI in employee engagement extends far beyond the current applications we've discussed. Through my research and conversations with industry leaders, I'm seeing emerging trends that suggest a fundamental shift in how organizations will use AI to foster connection and drive performance.

Consider the emergence of what I call "predictive engagement platforms." These sophisticated systems don't just measure current engagement levels; they anticipate potential disengagement before it occurs. At Innovation Tech, their AI system recently identified a pattern of declining engagement among high-performing developers months before it would have become apparent through traditional methods. By analyzing subtle changes in communication patterns, project involvement, and peer interactions, the system enabled proactive interventions that preserved both talent and team dynamics.

The integration of virtual reality with AI presents another frontier for engagement. Organizations are beginning to experiment with immersive learning experiences that adapt in real-time to employee responses and learning styles. During my recent work with Global Healthcare, they piloted an AI-driven VR program for medical staff training. The system didn't just present information; it created personalized scenarios based on each participant's role, experience level, and previous performance, fundamentally transforming how their teams learned and collaborated.

However, the most profound shift I'm observing involves what I term "collaborative AI," which are systems designed to enhance rather than replace human interaction. These tools don't just process data; they facilitate deeper human connections by identifying opportunities for meaningful collaboration across organizational boundaries. At Metropolitan Services, their AI platform analyzes project requirements and team member capabilities to suggest cross-functional collaborations that might otherwise never occur.

The key to successfully navigating this future lies in maintaining what I call the "human-tech equilibrium," ensuring that as AI capabilities expand, they enhance rather than diminish the fundamental human elements of work. This requires organizational leaders to think critically about not just what AI can do, but what it should do to create more engaging, fulfilling workplace experiences.

• • •

The transition to an AI-enhanced workplace requires a deliberate approach that prioritizes human development alongside technological advancement. Through my research with organizations navigating this evolution, I've identified several critical success factors that determine whether AI implementation strengthens or strains employee engagement.

The concept of "digital readiness" extends beyond basic technological literacy. At Financial Partners International, their preparation for AI integration began not with technical training but with what they called "future-state visioning." Teams spent time understanding how AI would enhance their roles rather than replace them. This approach transformed initial resistance into enthusiastic adoption, particularly when employees saw how AI could eliminate routine tasks and create space for more meaningful work.

Psychological preparation proves equally crucial. Organizations must acknowledge and address the natural anxiety that accompanies technological change. During my work with Advanced Manufacturing Corp, we discovered that employees' concerns about AI often stemmed from misconceptions about its capabilities. Their solution? Creating "AI exploration labs" where employees could experiment with new tools in a low-pressure environment, discovering firsthand how AI could augment their expertise rather than replace it.

The most successful organizations approach AI integration as a partnership between human insight and machine capability. Consider how Global Consulting transformed its project staffing process. Rather than allowing AI to make automated assignments, the company developed what it calls an "augmented staffing approach." Its AI system analyzes past project success patterns and team dynamics, but final decisions remain a collaborative process between managers and team members. This maintains human judgment while leveraging AI's pattern-recognition capabilities.

Perhaps most importantly, organizations must invest in what I term "adaptive expertise"—helping employees develop the flexibility to work effectively as AI capabilities evolve. This isn't about mastering specific tools but about cultivating the ability to navigate continuous technological change while maintaining human connections. At CoreTech Industries, they've embedded this principle into their learning and development framework, creating regular opportunities for employees to experiment with new AI applications while strengthening their interpersonal skills.

The future workplace won't be about humans versus machines, but about humans and machines creating new possibilities for engagement and achievement.

Practical Implementation: From AI Tools to Human Outcomes

The successful integration of AI into HR processes requires a structured, thoughtful approach that goes beyond simply adopting new technologies. Through my research and practical experience with organizations implementing AI solutions, I've developed what I call the "Strategic AI Integration Framework."

Before any organization implements AI tools for resume screening or engagement analysis, it must address fundamental strategic questions. At CoreTech Industries, their AI implementation initially faltered because they started with the solution rather than the problem. Their turnaround came when they stepped back and asked: "What specific organizational challenge are we trying to solve?" This simple but crucial question transformed their approach.

The RACI decision-making model proves particularly valuable in AI implementation. We used this framework at Global Manufacturing to clearly delineate roles: who was Responsible for implementation, who was Accountable for outcomes, who needed to be Consulted during the process, and who needed to be Informed of changes. This clarity prevented the common pitfall of unclear ownership and accountability.

Communication strategy becomes paramount when implementing AI solutions. Organizations must carefully consider not just what they communicate, but how and when they share information about AI initiatives. Atlantic Financial developed a multi-phase communication approach that addressed both the practical impacts of AI implementation and the emotional concerns of their workforce. They created what they called "Impact Maps" showing how AI tools would affect different roles and departments, ensuring transparency while maintaining engagement.

The true power of AI in HR lies not in automation alone, but in its ability to enhance human decision-making capabilities. Consider how predictive analytics can identify patterns in employee engagement data. However, the critical question becomes: What do we do with these insights? The most successful organizations use AI-generated insights as conversation starters rather than definitive answers. They create what I term "insight-action loops," where AI-identified patterns prompt human investigation and intervention.

Implementing AI: From Strategy to Execution

The successful implementation of AI initiatives requires what I call the "Strategic Integration Trinity": clear purpose, robust governance, and thoughtful change management. I've observed that success depends not on the sophistication of the AI tools themselves, but on how deliberately organizations approach their integration into existing systems and cultures.

At Global Financial Services, their initial AI implementation faltered despite substantial investment. The turning point came when they developed a comprehensive implementation framework centered on three critical questions: What organizational challenge are we addressing? How does this solution align with our desired culture? Who needs to be involved in the decision-making process?

Their revised approach began with stakeholder mapping using the RACI (Responsible, Accountable, Consulted, Informed) model. This seemingly simple tool transformed their implementation process by creating clear lines of accountability and communication channels. The Chief Technology Officer reflected, "We stopped treating AI implementation as a technical challenge and started approaching it as an organizational transformation initiative."

The Communication Cascade strategy represents a structured approach to sharing information about AI initiatives that address both practical and emotional aspects of technological change. Much like my grandmother's secret recipe that had to be shared in exactly the right order (trust me, mixing up the steps led to some memorable kitchen disasters), information should flow through an organization in a deliberate, organized way.

At Global Financial, we implemented this approach after their first attempt at communicating AI changes fell flat, and by flat, I mean it landed with all the grace of a lead balloon. Their initial mass email announcement about new AI tools left employees with more questions than answers and anxiety levels through the roof. The turnaround came when we restructured their communication approach. First, senior leadership communicated the strategic vision and purpose behind AI implementation. Next, middle managers received detailed information about specific impacts on their teams, along with tools and talking points for addressing common concerns. Finally, individual team members learned about concrete changes to their daily work, with clear timelines and support resources.

The Cascade proved transformative because it addressed both the "what" and the "so what" of AI implementation. When department heads could clearly explain how AI tools would eliminate the mind-numbing task of manually screening thousands of resumes, suddenly those same tools that had seemed threatening became welcome allies. By the time front-line managers were discussing specific changes with their teams, the conversation had shifted from "Will AI take my job?" to "How can AI help me do my job better?"

Through longitudinal studies of AI implementations, I've found that organizations often underestimate the importance of what I call "cultural readiness assessment." Before implementing any AI solution, successful organizations evaluate their cultural capacity for technological change, identifying potential resistance points and developing targeted strategies to address them.

The Bottom Line

AI doesn't need to replace the human touch—it needs to enhance it. Success comes from using AI to surface human nuance at scale, creating insights that prompt better human conversations, not shortcut them. The goal is human-AI collaboration, not replacement.

The Three AI Pathways to Engagement

1. Personalized Learning Experiences

AI creates adaptive learning journeys that respond to individual needs:

- Customized skill development paths based on role and learning style

- Real-time feedback and progress tracking

- Growth mindset acceleration through tailored challenges

- Learning partnerships that complement human mentorship

2. Enhanced HR Processes

AI transforms the employee lifecycle while preserving human connection:

- Smarter recruitment and onboarding experiences

- Real-time sentiment analysis and feedback processing

- Predictive engagement analytics that spot issues early

- Automated routine tasks that free humans for meaningful work

3. Predictive Analytics for Proactive Action

AI identifies patterns humans might miss:

- Early warning systems for disengagement

- Sentiment shifts over time (frustration → disappointment)

- Hidden engagement drivers (meeting times, workload patterns)

- Cross-team collaboration opportunities

Immediate Actions You Can Take Today

Ask the Right Questions Before Implementation

Strategic clarity prevents digital furniture:

- What are we hoping to learn that we don't already know?

- How will this information influence decisions or policies?

- Who will own the follow-up and action planning?

- What will success look like in 6 months? 12 months?

Conduct a Cultural Readiness Assessment

Before implementing any AI solution:

- Evaluate your organization's capacity for technological change

- Identify potential resistance points and concerns

- Assess current data privacy and governance frameworks

- Map stakeholder groups and their readiness levels

Implement the Communication Cascade

Structured approach to sharing AI initiatives:

Phase 1: Senior Leadership

- **Communicate strategic vision and purpose**

- **Address "why now" and organizational benefits**

- **Set expectations for change management process**

Phase 2: Middle Management

- Provide detailed impact information for their teams

- Equip with talking points for common concerns

- Clarify their role in supporting implementation

Phase 3: Front-line Teams

- Share concrete changes to daily work

- Provide clear timelines and support resources

- Focus on "how this helps you do your job better"

Use RACI for AI Implementation

Clear accountability prevents implementation chaos:

- **Responsible**: Who's doing the actual work of implementation?

- **Accountable**: Who's ultimately responsible for success/failure?

- **Consulted**: Who needs to provide input during the process?

- **Informed**: Who needs to know about changes and progress?

Open-Text + AI vs. Traditional Surveys

Aspect	Checkbox Surveys	Open-Text + AI Analysis
Depth of Insight	Shallow, pre-defined responses	Rich, nuanced employee voice
Bias Risk	High – limits to anticipated responses	Lower – employees speak authentically
Emotion Detection	None or inferred from scales	Identifies emotional tone and shifts
Surprise Factors	Rare – only get what you ask	High – unexpected themes emerge
Actionability	Often vague ("improve communication")	Specific insights about what and where

Practical AI Applications for Engagement

Real-Time Feedback Analysis

- Natural language processing of employee comments
- Sentiment tracking across teams and time periods
- Theme identification without predetermined categories
- Early warning signals for engagement drops

Personalized Development

- AI-driven learning recommendations based on role and goals
- Skill gap analysis with targeted learning paths
- Progress tracking that adapts to individual learning styles
- Connection to human mentors and development conversations

Enhanced Human Connection

- Smart scheduling for optimal collaboration opportunities
- Cross-functional project suggestions based on skills and interests
- Meeting optimization to reduce conflicts with personal priorities
- "Coffee roulette" pairings based on complementary backgrounds

Predictive Engagement Platforms

- Pattern recognition for potential disengagement
- Risk scoring based on multiple engagement indicators
- Proactive intervention recommendations
- Success tracking for different intervention strategies

Ethical AI Implementation Framework

Privacy and Transparency

- Clear policies on data collection and usage
- Employee consent and understanding of AI applications
- Regular audits for bias and fairness
- Transparent communication about AI capabilities and limitations

Governance Structure

- Cross-functional AI ethics committee
- Regular assessment of AI impact on employee experience
- Clear escalation paths for AI-related concerns
- Continuous monitoring and adjustment protocols

Human-Centered Metrics

- Track both efficiency gains and human impact measures
- Monitor stress levels alongside productivity improvements
- Assess quality of human interactions in AI-enhanced processes
- Evaluate depth and effectiveness of personalized experiences

Warning Signs Your AI Implementation is Failing

Technology-First Symptoms:

- Implementing AI tools without clear business problems to solve
- Measuring only efficiency gains, ignoring human impact
- Treating AI insights as definitive answers rather than conversation starters
- Creating "digital furniture" that looks impressive but adds no value

Human Element Failures:

- Employees report feeling surveilled rather than supported
- AI recommendations consistently ignored by managers
- Increased anxiety about job security and privacy
- Decreased human interaction and relationship quality

Communication Breakdowns:

- Lack of transparency about AI capabilities and limitations
- No clear accountability for AI-generated insights
- Resistance from managers who don't understand or trust AI outputs
- Employees feeling excluded from AI-related decisions

The Strategic AI Integration Framework

Phase 1: Foundation Setting (Months 1-2)

- Define specific organizational challenges AI will address
- Establish governance and ethical guidelines
- Conduct cultural readiness assessment
- Map stakeholders and communication strategy

Phase 2: Pilot Implementation (Months 3-6)

- Start with low-risk, high-impact applications
- Gather continuous feedback from pilot participants
- Refine processes based on early learnings
- Build internal AI literacy and comfort

Phase 3: Scaled Deployment (Months 7-12)

- Expand successful pilot programs
- Integrate AI insights into regular management processes
- Develop ongoing training and support systems
- Establish measurement and continuous improvement cycles

Future-State Visioning Questions

For Leadership:

- How will AI enhance our ability to create meaningful work experiences?
- What human capabilities do we want to amplify, not replace?
- How will we maintain organizational culture as AI becomes more prevalent?

For Employees:

- How might AI eliminate routine tasks to create space for more meaningful work?

- What new skills will be most valuable in an AI-enhanced workplace?
- How can AI help you better connect with colleagues and contribute to team success?

For HR Professionals:
- How will AI change our role from administrative to strategic?
- What new competencies do we need to develop to effectively leverage AI?
- How do we ensure AI enhances rather than diminishes human connection?

Remember: The Human-Tech Equilibrium

Successful AI implementation maintains balance:
- **Technology** provides insights and eliminates routine work
- **Humans** make decisions, build relationships, and create meaning
- **Together** they create more engaging, fulfilling workplace experiences

Key Principle: AI should make people more human at work, not less. Use it to surface patterns, facilitate connections, and create space for the uniquely human elements of work—creativity, empathy, and authentic relationship building.

Success Metrics for AI-Enhanced Engagement

Quantitative Measures:
- Employee engagement scores pre/post AI implementation
- Time-to-insight on engagement issues
- Manager confidence in data-driven decisions
- Employee adoption rates of AI-enhanced tools

Qualitative Indicators:
- Quality of development conversations
- Depth of manager-employee relationships
- Employee trust in organizational decision-making
- Innovation and creative problem-solving increases

Bottom line: AI's greatest contribution to engagement isn't replacing human judgment—it's enhancing our ability to see, understand, and respond to what people really need to thrive at work.

*"Our industry does not respect tradition—
it only respects innovation."*
– Satya Nadella

CHAPTER 9

Moving Forward: What's Next for Engagement?

There's a saying in HR: Some people grow into leadership, and others are thrown into it and handed a match. I met Clark during one of the more combustible moments in his career.

At the time, we were working together at a Wealth Management firm that was structured into specialized research departments by asset class—real estate, private equity, and hedge funds. Clark led one of those research teams. He was smart, dedicated, and personally well-liked. He always remembered people's birthdays, stayed late to finish decks, and gave 110%. But he was also deeply overwhelmed and unintentionally overwhelming to others.

He struggled with delegation. Not because he didn't trust his team, exactly, but because he was afraid that if anything went sideways, it would all come back to him. So, he did what many new managers do: he micromanaged. He would ask for a draft, rewrite most of it himself, and then stay up until midnight tweaking the font size. Team meetings were often one-way updates. His analysts didn't feel seen. His associates didn't feel supported. And nobody knew what success looked like—only that their work had to be perfect and submitted on time.

Eventually, I started noticing the signs: hallway check-ins, anonymous comments in surveys, whispers of burnout, and "managing up" as survival. Turnover on his team ticked up. A few promising junior hires left after less than a year.

But the thing was, Clark wasn't a bad person. He wasn't even a bad manager in the classic sense. He just hadn't been taught how to lead people—how to set expectations, give feedback, manage his anxiety, or build trust beyond task lists. He had been promoted for his technical expertise, not his people skills. A story as old as corporate time.

Leadership considered letting him go.

Instead, they made a different move. They transitioned him to a new role in portfolio management—client-facing, faster-paced, and less hierarchical. And critically, they paired him with a seasoned manager who had a reputation for directness and support in equal measure. I stayed involved, coaching him through the shift, helping him reframe what leadership could look like.

That's when things started to change.

At first, Clark was skeptical. The old patterns didn't die easily. In one of our first coaching sessions, he said, "I just don't want to let anything fall through the cracks."

To which I replied: "If you're the only net, everyone else will stop catching."

He started experimenting with delegation. Small at first: assigning a junior associate to lead a client follow-up call, asking for input before finalizing a pitch deck. Then bigger: trusting his team to own deliverables from start to finish. Was it perfect? No. But it didn't have to be.

His new manager helped, too. He gave him straight feedback without sugarcoating, and he modeled how to hold people accountable without scaring them into silence. Instead of asking "Why isn't this done yet?" the manager asked, "What support do you need to move this forward?" Clark took notes. Literally.

And something remarkable happened.

He softened without losing his edge. He became more confident and less controlling. His team meetings opened up. He started asking questions like, "What's getting in your way?" and "Where do you want to grow this quarter?" He got more comfortable saying, "I don't know," and more consistent in giving timely, thoughtful feedback.

One of his former teammates said to me months later, "He's like a different person. He actually listens now."

But here's what I found most powerful: he didn't just get better, he started helping others get better. He mentored a junior analyst through her first major client presentation. He created a shared resource folder to reduce last-minute scrambling. He even launched a peer-coaching lunch group with two other managers who admitted they'd also been faking their way through feedback conversations for years.

Over time, Clark became one of the most trusted people in the department. Not just for his technical knowledge, but for his ability to lead calmly, clearly, and with a sense of care. He stayed with the organization for another seven years. His team stabilized. His client reviews were glowing. And he became the kind of manager people requested to work with.

And all of this happened because someone—actually, a few someones—decided not to write him off.

That's the real point of this story. "Moving forward" doesn't always mean making radical changes or clearing the decks. Sometimes it means seeing people as works in progress. It means giving them feedback that's real, support that's targeted, and space to evolve.

Clark's transformation was his own work. We simply created the conditions for him to grow.

That's what healthy organizations do. They don't just measure performance, they build potential. They don't just promote top performers, they develop better leaders. And they understand that talent isn't static. People are not fixed assets. They're dynamic, layered, and often messy, just like culture.

In a lot of ways, Clark's transformation mirrored what I wish more organizations would invest in: long-view leadership. Not quick wins, not performance theater, but meaningful development. The kind that starts with awareness, continues through challenge, and shows up in the way people treat each other every day.

And no, it doesn't always work out. Some people aren't ready. Some won't do the work. But far more often than we think, the issue isn't with them. They're just unsupported. Or miscast. Or stuck in a system that rewards silence over growth.

• • •

The question is: What if we assumed people could get better? What if our default wasn't "cut the weak link" but "coach the potential"?

Clark taught me something I've carried into every client conversation since: Talent development is leadership development. And both are built on the same foundation of clarity, care, and a willingness to believe that people can change.

Because they can. If we let them.

• • •

The landscape of employee engagement has shifted dramatically since I began my research in this field. As we look toward the future, one thing becomes crystal clear: the old engagement playbook needs a complete rewrite. Organizations can't continue approaching engagement with pre-pandemic thinking and tools from an era when work-life balance was more buzzword than business imperative.

Through my recent work with organizations navigating this transformation, I've observed three critical shifts that will define the future of engagement. First, artificial intelligence and machine learning are revolutionizing how we understand and measure engagement in real-time. Second, we're seeing a fundamental reimagining of performance management and professional development. Third, and perhaps most critically, organizations are being forced to reconcile their operational needs with employees' evolving expectations about work-life integration.

The days of annual engagement surveys and one-size-fits-all development plans are behind us. Today's workforce demands—and technology enables—a more nuanced, personalized, and holistic approach to engagement. The organizations that thrive will be those that embrace this evolution while maintaining the human connection at the heart of meaningful work.

Reimagining the Organizational-Employee Contract

Let me share a story that perfectly illustrates this transformation. At Metropolitan Health, a crisis was brewing. Their talented clinicians were burning out at unprecedented rates, threatening both patient care quality and organizational stability. The traditional response would have been to throw more wellness programs at the problem or increase compensation. Instead, they did something radical: they completely reimagined their care delivery model.

Working directly with their medical teams, they developed what they called "flexibility pods," or small groups of clinicians who collectively managed patient care while supporting each other's need for genuine work-life integration. The results were remarkable. Not only did burnout rates plummet, but patient satisfaction scores increased. Why? Because well-rested, engaged healthcare providers deliver better care.

Global Financial provides another instructive example of balancing organizational needs with employee well-being. Facing high turnover in their technology division, they discovered their traditional 9-5 structure was driving away top talent. Their solution? They implemented what I call "performance-based flexibility"—measuring outcomes rather than hours spent at a desk. The twist? They didn't just allow flexibility; they actively encouraged it by training managers to focus on results rather than face time.

Practical Strategies for Transformation

Based on these and other case studies, I've identified several concrete steps organizations can take to begin this transformation:

Start with honest dialogue. Pacific Technologies initiated what they called "future of work conversations" across all levels of their organization. These weren't just feel-good sessions but structured discussions about specific pain points and potential solutions. The key was creating psychological safety for employees to express their real needs without fear of repercussion.

Redefine productivity metrics. Organizations need to move beyond traditional productivity measurements. Companies can develop "impact metrics," measuring not just what employees do but the actual value they create. This shift fundamentally changed how managers approached team oversight and how employees viewed their own contributions.

Create intentional flexibility. This goes beyond simply allowing remote work. It means designing systems that actively support different work patterns while ensuring business continuity. Global Manufacturing achieved this by mapping their core business needs against employee preferences, creating what they called "flexibility zones," or periods when presence was crucial versus times when individual scheduling could prevail.

Build support infrastructure. Real change requires robust support systems. Tech Forward revolutionized their approach by creating what they call "flexibility facilitators"—trained professionals who help teams navigate new working arrangements while ensuring business objectives are met.

The most successful organizations recognize that this isn't about choosing between business needs and employee wellbeing; it's about finding creative ways to advance both simultaneously. When organizations get this right, they create what I call a "virtuous cycle of engagement," where satisfied employees drive better business outcomes, which in turn enables more investment in employee success.

Questioning Our Organizational Assumptions

One of the most valuable exercises I've encountered in my work with organizations comes from the Toyota Production System's 'Five Whys' approach,[25] which I've adapted into what I call the 'Seven Whys' method." When Pacific Technologies struggled with its return-to-office mandate, we applied this method to challenge the company's basic assumptions. "Why do we need people in the office?" led to "Why do we believe collaboration only happens face-to-face?" which led to "Why haven't we invested in better digital collaboration tools?" Each question peeled back another layer of unconscious bias about work.

This questioning process often reveals uncomfortable truths. At Global Financial, the leadership team discovered their insistence on office presence stemmed more from comfort with traditional management approaches than actual business necessity. This realization led them to completely reimagine their workspace strategy, creating what they call "purpose-driven presence"—being in the office when it truly adds value, not just because of tradition.

---

25 Liker, J. K. (2004). The Toyota Way: 14 Management Principles from the World's Greatest Manufacturer. McGraw-Hill.

Generational Shifts: Understanding Without Surrendering

The arrival of Generation Z in the workforce has sparked countless discussions about changing workplace expectations. However, I've observed that focusing solely on generational differences can blind us to universal engagement drivers. During my work with Tech Forward, we discovered something fascinating: their Gen Z employees weren't asking for anything radically different. They were just more vocal about the same human needs that previous generations often suppressed.

This doesn't mean organizations should ignore generational perspectives. Rather, they need to find what I call the "engagement sweet spot," where fundamental human needs meet modern workplace expectations. Innovation Corp achieved this by creating multi-generational design teams for their workplace policies. Instead of assuming what different generations wanted, they facilitated dialogues that revealed surprising commonalities in need for flexibility, purpose, and recognition.

The key isn't to completely reorganize around any single generation's preferences, but to understand how different groups express universal engagement drivers. For instance, while a Baby Boomer might view career development through the lens of vertical progression, a Gen Z employee might prioritize skill acquisition across various roles. The core need for growth remains the same; it's the expression that differs.

Circling Back:
The Fundamentals of Future Engagement

As we look toward the future of engagement, we must return to some fundamental questions that many organizations still struggle to answer. Through my work with companies attempting to transform their engagement strategies, I've observed that success often hinges on their willingness to honestly confront these essential challenges.

Take Global Manufacturing's recent transformation effort. Their leadership team spent months developing sophisticated engagement initiatives before realizing they'd missed a crucial first step: aligning their DEI goals with core operational processes. Their compensation and promotion practices told a different story from their stated values about inclusion. As one senior leader admitted to me, "We were building a beautiful house on a shaky foundation."

The concept of psychological safety—the ability to take risks without fear of retribution[26]—remains paramount. Metropolitan Health discovered this when they investigated why their innovation initiatives weren't gaining traction. Despite extensive resources and support, employees remained hesitant to challenge existing processes. Their solution? They created what they called "Challenge Labs"—designated forums where questioning current practices wasn't just permitted but celebrated.

Leadership development in the engagement space requires particular attention. At Tech Forward, they realized their leaders had plenty of access to engagement data but lacked understanding of how to translate that information into meaningful action. They

---

26 Edmondson, A. C. (2018). The Fearless Organization: Creating Psychological Safety in the Workplace for Learning, Innovation, and Growth. John Wiley & Sons.

developed what I call "engagement learning loops," where leaders receive information, implement changes, and get rapid feedback on the impact of their efforts. This practical approach transformed abstract engagement concepts into tangible leadership behaviors.

The question of feedback and growth deserves special attention. Innovation Corp revolutionized their approach by moving from traditional performance reviews to what they term "growth conversations." These discussions focus not just on what employees have achieved but on how they can develop their capabilities. The key difference? Feedback becomes a tool for development rather than just evaluation.

Understanding threshold attributes—those fundamental characteristics that define success in your organization—becomes increasingly critical as work environments evolve. Pacific Technologies learned this lesson when they discovered their definition of success hadn't evolved with their hybrid work model. They needed to redefine what high performance looks like when traditional visibility metrics no longer apply.

The Bottom Line

The future of engagement isn't about radical overhauls—it's about seeing people as works in progress and creating conditions for growth. Success comes from assuming people can get better, then building systems that support their development rather than writing them off.

The Three Critical Shifts Defining Future Engagement

1. AI-Enhanced Real-Time Understanding

- Move from annual surveys to continuous sentiment monitoring

- Use machine learning to identify engagement patterns before they become problems

- Leverage predictive analytics to address team dynamics proactively

- Create personalized engagement strategies based on individual needs and preferences

2. Reimagined Performance and Development

- Shift from time-based to impact-based productivity measures

- Replace annual reviews with ongoing "growth conversations"

- Focus on building capabilities, not just evaluating past performance

- Develop threshold attributes that align with evolving work environments

3. Work-Life Integration Revolution

- Balance organizational needs with employee expectations for flexibility
- Create "purpose-driven presence" rather than mandated office time
- Design support systems that enable different work patterns
- Build business models that thrive on outcomes, not oversight

Immediate Actions You Can Take Today

Challenge Your Organizational Assumptions

Use the "Seven Whys" approach to uncover unconscious biases:

Start with basic questions:

- Why do we need people in the office?
- Why do we measure productivity this way?
- Why do we structure teams like this?
- Why do we promote certain people?

Dig deeper with each answer:

- Why do we believe collaboration only happens face-to-face?
- Why haven't we invested in better digital tools?
- Why are we comfortable with traditional management approaches?
- Why do we assume presence equals productivity?

Build the Foundation for Future Engagement

Align Values with Operations:

- Audit compensation and promotion practices against stated Connection and Belonging goals

- Ensure engagement initiatives reflect actual organizational values

- Create transparency between what you say and what you reward

Establish Psychological Safety:

- Create opportunities where questioning current practices is celebrated

- Reward constructive dissent and innovative thinking

- Make it safe to admit mistakes and learn from them

- Encourage experimentation without fear of retribution

Transform Your Measurement Approach

Develop Impact Metrics:

- **Future-focused**: Value created, problems solved, relationships built

- **Outcome-based**: Results achieved, goals met, improvements made

- **Growth-oriented**: Skills developed, others supported, innovations contributed

Create Engagement Learning Loops:

- **Gather**: Collect engagement data through multiple channels

- **Analyze**: Identify patterns and priority areas for action

- **Act**: Implement targeted interventions

- **Measure**: Track impact of changes on engagement

- **Adjust**: Refine approach based on results

Implement Future-Ready Leadership Development

Coach the Potential Mindset:

- Default to "coach the potential" rather than "cut the weak link"

- Invest in long-view leadership development

- Provide targeted support for struggling managers

- Create cohort based circles for shared learning

Growth Conversation Framework: Instead of traditional performance reviews, focus on:

- **Strengths**: What are you naturally good at?

- **Growth areas**: Where do you want to develop?

- **Support needed**: How can we help you succeed?

- **Future vision**: Where do you see yourself going?

- **Next steps**: What specific actions will move you forward?

CHAPTER 9 MOVING FORWARD: WHAT'S NEXT FOR ENGAGEMENT? TEAR SHEET

Generational Integration Strategy

Find the Engagement Sweet Spot

Universal needs expressed differently across generations:

- **Career Development**: Vertical progression (Boomers) vs. Skill acquisition (Gen Z)

- **Recognition**: Formal acknowledgment vs. Real-time feedback

- **Communication**: Email/meetings vs. Teams/video calls

- **Work-Life Balance**: Separation vs. Integration

Multi-Generational Design Principles

- Create policy design teams with representatives from different generations

- Facilitate dialogues to reveal commonalities in core needs

- Focus on universal engagement drivers while accommodating different expressions

- Avoid assumptions about what different groups want—ask them directly

Essential Future Engagement Elements

Psychological Safety Foundations

- **Challenge current practices**: Make questioning the status quo a valued behavior
- **Normalize learning**: Treat mistakes as development opportunities
- **Encourage vulnerability**: Leaders model admitting uncertainty
- **Reward innovation**: Celebrate creative problem-solving attempts

Continuous Learning Culture

- **Skill-based advancement**: Promote based on capabilities, not just tenure
- **Cross-functional exposure**: Create opportunities to learn outside your area
- **Peer teaching**: Encourage knowledge sharing across teams
- **Learning time**: Dedicated hours for skill development and growth

Adaptive Leadership Capabilities

- **Data interpretation**: Turn engagement insights into actionable strategies
- **Inclusive decision-making**: Seek diverse perspectives before major choices
- **Cultural navigation**: Understand and bridge generational and cultural differences
- **Change facilitation**: Help teams adapt to evolving work environments

Warning Signs You're Stuck in Old Engagement Models

Outdated Thinking Patterns:

- Measuring productivity by presence rather than results

- Using one-size-fits-all engagement strategies

- Relying solely on annual surveys for engagement data

- Assuming generational stereotypes instead of asking individuals

- Treating flexibility as a privilege rather than a strategic advantage

Structural Problems:

- Promotion and compensation practices contradict stated values

- Leadership development focuses on technical skills over people skills

- Performance management emphasizes evaluation over development

- Decision-making processes exclude diverse perspectives

Support systems designed for in-person work only

Remember: The Clark Principle

People are not fixed assets—they're dynamic, layered, and capable of growth.

Key insights from successful transformations:

- Provide feedback that's real, support that's targeted, and space to evolve

- Create conditions for growth rather than trying to "fix" people

- Invest in long-view leadership development, not quick fixes

- Build potential while measuring performance

- Assume people can get better, then prove it through your systems

The question that changes everything: What if our default wasn't "cut the weak link" but "coach the potential"?

Bottom line: The future of engagement belongs to organizations that see people as works in progress and build systems that help them become their best professional selves.

"Do the best you can until you know better.
Then, when you know better, do better."
– MAYA ANGELOU

What I'd Tell
My Younger Self

If I could sit down with my 25-year-old self—the one who wore shoulder pads like armor and thought sheer effort could fix any workplace—I'd probably start with this:

You are not going to save the world.
At least, not in the way you think you will.

When I was younger, I had big, idealistic goals. I was going to change organizations. Transform cultures. Make work better for everyone. You know, just a typical Tuesday.

And then life happened.

I hit the point in my career—what I jokingly call my "Come to G-d moment"—when I realized I couldn't control everything. I couldn't fix every system. I couldn't protect every employee from every terrible manager or every organization from its worst habits.

And in that moment, I asked myself: *If I can't change the whole world . . . why bother?*

But here's the thing: the smaller, quieter work does matter.

I've had former employees stop me years later and say, "You helped me see something in myself I hadn't seen before." I've gotten notes from people who said my coaching changed how they saw their own worth. There was one woman named Lillian who left me a handwritten letter the day she moved on to a new role. She wrote about the ways I'd made her feel capable, visible, and valued.

I kept that letter in my notebook for years.

And I'd pull it out in the hard seasons. When the work felt invisible. When I wondered if anything I was doing made a difference.

What I'd tell my younger self is this:

Keep going.

Keep showing up with care.

Keep doing the small things.

Because they ripple.

Even when you don't see it.

• • •

Looking back now, if I could package up a few hard-won truths and mail them back to that idealistic, slightly overwhelmed younger version of me, along with maybe a better pair of work shoes and a stiff tequila drink, I know exactly what I'd say.

First: Perfection is a trap.

There's this idea, especially early in your career, that if you just get everything right, things will fall into place. That the organization will reward you, that your team will respect you, that people won't question your judgment. I clung to that idea for years. I edited every email five times. I created policies that were airtight and soulless. I tried to control outcomes by pre-solving problems before they even had a chance to breathe.

And still, I messed up. A lot.

It was early in my career—too early, frankly—to be managing people without at least a minor in diplomacy. I was trying to be the kind of leader who brought warmth and humanity into the workplace, mostly because I had worked under enough robots-in-blazers to know I didn't want to become one. I wanted to be the manager people liked. Someone people trusted. Someone who made the workplace feel a little more human.

And then I opened my mouth.

I was in the middle of a conversation with a junior employee— one I liked, one I truly respected—and in a moment of what I thought was encouragement, I said something that still makes me cringe 25 years later.

I called her "my pet."

Now, in my head, this was affectionate. British even. Quaint! Endearing! Something Maggie Smith would mutter in *Downton Abbey* with a sip of tea and a raised eyebrow.

But it wasn't.

It was weird. It was demeaning. It was the exact opposite of empowering. And it landed like a lead balloon. Definitely not the vibe I was going for.

Worse? My boss overheard it.

He pulled me aside later that day and, with a look somewhere between horror and disbelief, asked, "What the hell were you thinking?" (Okay, that's the sanitized version. I believe the exact quote was more like, "What the f#*k is wrong with you?")

. . .

"I meant it as a compliment," I said, scrambling to explain, as if intent could magically undo the damage.

That's when the real lesson hit me: Intent is not impact.

It doesn't matter that I meant well. What mattered was how it made her feel. And I can guarantee she did not feel seen, empowered, or appreciated at that moment. She felt objectified, turned into a mascot instead of a mentee. That was my wake-up call.

It was also a masterclass in what not to do as a leader. You don't get to build trust by being charming. You build it by being clear, consistent, and careful with your words. You don't get to make up for a power imbalance with faux familiarity. You level the playing field with transparency and real respect.

For years afterward, I replayed that moment like a bad sitcom rerun, especially on sleepless nights when the inner critic decided to throw a greatest-hits montage of my most cringeworthy career missteps. But with time and a fair amount of therapy, I learned to treat that moment not as an indictment but as information. I made a mistake. It doesn't mean I am a mistake.

What it does mean is that I have a responsibility to do better. To own it. To apologize, if needed. To adjust. And to never, ever use terms of endearment in the workplace again unless they're backed by a collective bargaining agreement or a decades-long friendship.

What I didn't know then, but know now, is that leadership is not about being flawless. It's about being human. And humans say dumb things sometimes. But the question isn't whether you've messed up. It's whether you're willing to reflect, repair, and move forward with more humility than you started with.

So, if you ever find yourself mentally screaming, "What the hell was I thinking?", take a breath. You're not alone. You're just learning. And that's what leaders do.

That moment, mortifying as it was, taught me something I've carried with me ever since: When you mess up, you don't double down. You own it, you adjust, and you move forward. That's not just good crisis management, it's leadership. People don't expect perfection. But they do expect you to be honest, resilient, and human.

This lesson took me longer to learn than I'd like to admit. I used to think that if my heart was in the right place, if I meant to support someone, or meant to build a better culture, then I should get credit for that. Gold star. Participation trophy.

But people don't experience your intent. They experience your behavior.

I remember once rolling out a company-wide feedback tool designed to promote transparency. It was smart, scalable, and in my mind, deeply supportive of growth. Within days, the quiet backlash started. Employees weren't feeling supported, they were feeling watched. They were anxious, confused, and in some cases, offended. I'd built a system that aligned with my values, but I hadn't stopped to ask how it would land in the context of theirs.

So, I listened. I asked more questions. I sat in uncomfortable conversations where people told me, directly, that the thing I built to help them made them feel small. And then I changed it. Not because I was wrong in intent but because they were right in experience.

These are the moments that separate well-meaning leaders from meaningful ones.

Next, and maybe most importantly, focus on the humans.

Behind every title, every performance rating, every frustrating reply-all thread is a person. Someone with rent to pay, a complicated relationship with their dad, a dream they haven't spoken out loud yet, and a desire, sometimes buried, to do good work.

In my early years, I was so focused on policy and systems and fairness-by-structure that I forgot to make room for people. I once coached a manager who was struggling with an underperforming employee. We went over goals, metrics, and communication styles, but something still wasn't adding up. Finally, I asked, "Have you just . . . checked in on her? As a person?" He hadn't. When he did, he learned she was caring for a sick parent and drowning in guilt over letting her team down. That one conversation unlocked compassion, reengagement, and a plan. Not because the performance changed overnight, but because the relationship did.

It's easy to get lost in frameworks and KPIs. But at the end of the day, work is human. Leadership is human. And if you forget that, you're going to lose people. Maybe not immediately, but eventually and meaningfully.

And finally, the big stuff is built from small stuff.

• • •

I used to think that culture change came from bold moves like executive mandates, org-wide initiatives, and keynote speeches with decent coffee. And those have their place. But what I've seen again and again is the things that change people's experience of work happen in the day-to-day.

It's the manager who says, "You were quiet in that meeting; what's your take?"

The team that revises their meeting schedule so working parents don't have to choose between visibility and daycare pickup.

The HR lead who pushes back on the "culture fit" hire because it's code for "someone like us."

The leader who says, "I got that wrong, and here's what I'm doing differently."

That's the work. Not the flashy stuff. The repetition. The consistency. The moments when no one's watching.

Trust doesn't come from one training. Inclusion doesn't come from a slide deck. Belonging doesn't come from a quarterly town hall. These things are earned, again and again, in the hallway, on Zoom, in the Teams thread, in the moment where you pause and decide to listen instead of defending yourself.

If I could go back and whisper all this into my own ear, if I could hand my younger self a kind but honest roadmap, I wouldn't point her to a better strategy. I'd tell her to get more comfortable being wrong, to stay open longer, and to give people more credit than she thinks they've earned.

Because that's what makes the difference.

And that's what will move us all forward.

About the Author

Dr. Rosalind F. Cohen, SPHR, SHRM-SCP, is a New York native who's spent over 25 years figuring out why workplaces can be so wonderfully terrible—and more importantly, how to fix them. After moving around the country more times than she cares to count (seriously, the boxes never fully got unpacked), she became something of an expert on belonging and connection. Turns out, all that searching for "home" was excellent preparation for helping organizations create places where people actually want to work.

Currently serving as Chief People Officer at Laird Norton Wetherby, she leads with curiosity and empathy to build cultures where team members feel valued for their unique contributions. She also founded Socius Strategies, where she partners with companies to build cultures where people thrive instead of just survive. Her approach blends social psychology, industrial psychology, and a healthy dose of "let's cut the BS and make this actually work." She holds a Ph.D. in Leadership and Change from Antioch University, where she researched the not-so-mysterious connections between inclusive leadership and employee engagement. Spoiler alert: when people feel like they belong, they do better work.

Throughout her career, Dr. Cohen has built HR functions at organizations including The Walt Disney Family Museum, Hall Capital Partners, and Nollenberger Capital Partners. She's designed talent strategies, led DEIB initiatives, and somehow convinced leaders that treating people well is actually good for business. Her colleagues describe her as "badass"—a title she wears with pride, especially since it's way better than "traditional HR lady."

When she's not revolutionizing workplace culture, you'll find her traveling the world or hanging out with her two adult kids, whom she adores (even when they ignore her texts). Her work is guided by the Jewish principle of *tikkun olam*—repairing the world—which she does one radically connected workplace at a time.

Dr. Cohen believes in bold ideas, authentic leadership, and the radical notion that work doesn't have to suck. She's here to help organizations create the kind of culture where everyone can bring their whole selves to work—quirks, strengths, and all.

For more information or to contact the author visit:

DrRozCohen.com

www.ingramcontent.com/pod-product-compliance
Lightning Source LLC
Chambersburg PA
CBHW071158210326
41597CB00016B/1589